Changes and Conflicts

Changes and Conflicts:
Korean Immigrant Families in New York

Pyong Gap Min
Queens College of CUNY

Allyn and Bacon
Boston • London • Toronto • Sydney • Tokyo • Singapore

Series Editor: Sarah L. Kelbaugh
Vice President, Social Science: Karen Hanson
Series Editorial Assistant: Elissa V. Schaen
Marketing Manager: Karon Bowers
Consulting Editor: Sylvia Shepard
Manufacturing Buyer: Suzanne Lareau
Cover Administrator: Suzanne Harbison
Cover Designer: Jenny Hart
Editorial Production Service: Omegatype Typography, Inc.

 PEARSON CUSTOM PUBLISHING
75 Arlington Street, Boston, MA 02116
A Pearson Education Company

Internet: www.abacon.com
America Online: keyword: College Online

ISBN: 0-205-27455-2

Printed in the United States of America.
10   9   8   7   6   5   4   3   2   02   01   00   99   98

Contents

Foreword to the Series

The United States is now experiencing the largest wave of immigration in the country's history. The 1990s, it is predicted, will see more new immigrants enter the United States than in any decade in American history. New immigrants from Asia, Latin America, and the Caribbean are changing the American ethnic landscape.

Until recently, immigration was associated in the minds of many Americans with the massive influx of southern and eastern Europeans at the turn of the century. Since the late 1960s, America has again become a country of large-scale immigration, this time attracting newcomers from developing societies of the world. The number of foreign-born is at an all-time high: nearly 20 million foreign-born persons were counted in the 1990 census. Although immigrants are a smaller share of the nation's population than they were earlier in the century—8 percent in 1990 compared to about 15 percent in 1910—recent immigrants are having an especially dramatic impact because their geographic concentration is greater today. About half of all immigrants entering the United States during the 1980s moved to eight urban areas: Los Angeles, New York, Miami, Anaheim, Chicago, Washington, D.C., Houston, and San Francisco. America's major urban centers are, increasingly, immigrant cities with new ethnic mixes.

Who are the new immigrants? What are their lives like here? How are they redefining themselves and their cultures? And how are they contributing to a new and changing America? The *New Immigrants Series* provides a set of case studies that explores these themes among a variety of groups. Each book in the series is written by a recognized expert who has done extensive in-depth ethnographic research on one of the immigrant groups. The groups represent a broad range of today's arrivals, coming from a variety of countries and cultures. The studies cover a wide geographical range as well, based on research done in different parts of the country, from New York to California.

Most of the books in the series are written by anthropologists. All draw on qualitative research that shows what it means to be an immigrant in America today. As part of each study, individual immigrants tell their stories, which will help give a sense of the experiences and problems of the newcomers. Through the case studies, a dynamic picture emerges of the way immigrants are carving out new lives for themselves at the same time they are creating a new and more diverse America.

The ethnographic case study, long the anthropologist's trademark, provides a depth often lacking in research on immigrants in the United States. Many anthropologists, moreover, like a number of authors in the *New Immigrants Series*, have done research in the sending society as well as in the United States. Having field experience at both ends of the migration chain makes anthropologists particularly sensitive to the role of transnational ties that link immigrants to their home societies. With first-hand experience of immigrants in their home culture, anthropologists are also well positioned to appreciate continuities as well as changes in the immigrant setting.

As the United States faces a growing backlash against immigration, and many Americans express ambivalence and sometimes hostility toward the latest arrivals, it becomes more important than ever to learn about the new immigrants and to hear their voices. The case studies in the *New Immigrants Series* will help readers understand the cultures and lives of the newest Americans and bring out the complex ways the newcomers are coming to terms with and creatively adapting to life in a new land.

NANCY FONER
Series Editor

Acknowledgments

In the 1996 Fall term, I received the Queens College Presidential Research Award that gave me 100 percent release time. Although the research award was given to me to complete my book on Korean military comfort women, it helped me write much of this book as well. For Korean immigrant families in New York, I used results of several surveys as well as my ethnographic research. The surveys were funded by the 1988 Professional Staff Congress of the City University of New York Research Award, the 1989 Korean-American Research Foundation grant, the 1993 Ford Foundation diversity initiative grant, and the 1996 FIPSE grant.

My article on relations between Korean immigrant parents and their children, cited in this book several times, was based on data collected by my son, Jay, for his Westinghouse Science project in 1991. My wife, Hyun Suk, arranged interviews with several of her friends. She also provided valuable information about Korean immigrants' marital relations, which was incorporated into many pages of this book. Kwang Hee Kim, the former director of the Korean Family Counseling Center, offered me many stories about Korean immigrants' marital conflicts, which gave me insights into the sources of Koreans' marital conflicts. Dong Wan Joo, In Cha Kim, Joann Hong, Bong Ho Ha, and Soon Bong Lee helped me by telling stories of several Korean immigrant families they knew. Some of these stories are introduced in this book. Yoon Jung Oh, a new immigrant and a sociology major in Korea, read Chapter 3 and provided valuable comments. Mehdi Bozorgmehr and Alem Habtu, two of my best non-Korean friends, and Charles Jaret, my mentor at Georgia State University, have given me encouragement and support, which has been essential to completing this book as well as to my other research and professional activities.

Nancy Foner, the Editor of the *New Immigrant Series,* and Sylvia Shepard, the Anthropology Consulting Editor, edited two versions of this book manuscript carefully, but quickly. They also gave me many suggestions to make the book more interesting to lay readers. Without their effective editing, this book would not have been published in 1997. Further, I would not have started this book without their enthusiastic support from the beginning. In addition, I would like to acknowledge that I have learned a lot about ethnographic research from their suggestions and guidance.

My personal and telephone interviews with fifty Korean men, women, children, and elderly people compose the backbone of this book. Without their willingness to share their life experiences and others' stories with me, this book would have been impossible. My interviews with a dozen staff members of Korean ethnic organizations in New York and several surveys of Korean women, children, and elderly people also provide additional data sources for this book. This book would have been incomplete without data provided by the staff members of Korean ethnic organizations and the respondents to the surveys in New York.

I

Changes and Conflicts in Family Life

Chun Ho Kim, along with his wife and two children, immigrated to this country in 1988 at the age of 33. Like many other Koreans, Kim chose transpacific migration to give his children better opportunities for education. Attracted by the convenience of many Korean restaurants and Korean ethnic networks, he initially settled in Flushing, New York. A manager for a bank branch in Korea, Kim found his first job in his brother's green grocery store in Flushing, while his wife worked at a Korean-owned general merchandise store (selling items imported from Asia) in nearby Jamaica, the first job she ever had in her life. Five years ago, with private loans from his brother, Kim bought a Korean-owned general merchandise store in Brooklyn. Four years ago, they moved from Flushing to Bayside to send their children to better public schools. With after-school preparations in a cram school, both of their children were admitted to the Bronx High School of Science, the second best public high school in New York City. Their son is in the eleventh grade, and their daughter is in the ninth.

Since they started their own business, Mr. and Mrs Kim have worked together at the shop from 9:30 A.M. to 7:00 P.M., six days a week. Getting home at 8:00, Mrs. Kim usually prepares dinner while her husband reads a Korean daily newspaper and watches Korean TV programs. However, over the last two years Mrs. Kim has frequently argued with her husband over his not doing dishwashing and house cleaning. She complains: "I work in the store as many hours as you do, and I play an even more important role in our business than you. But you don't help me at home. It's never fair. My friends in Korea work full-time at home, but they at least don't have to work outside. Here I work too much both inside and outside the home. Did you bring me to this country for exploitation?"

Mr. Kim cannot understand how much and how quickly his wife has changed her attitude toward him since she came to this country. He does not remember her talking back to him in Korea. Yet recently she has not only talked back, but also often started arguments. To him, her accusation that he does nothing at home makes no sense. In addition to taking care of house maintenance, he often takes care of garbage disposal and helps his wife with grocery shopping, neither of which he did in Korea. Now his wife pushes him to do house cleaning and dishwashing. The image of a husband washing dishes in the kitchen is far from the ideal family pattern he dreamed of in Korea. Further, his teenaged children often talk back to him and do not show him the kind of respect that a middle-aged father usually gets from his teenaged children in Korea. He knows his friends in Korea exercise much more authority and power over their wives and children. He wonders what has gone wrong with him and his family since they came to the United States.

Many Korean immigrant families in New York experience marital and generational conflicts similar to the Kim family. However, the mainstream media have paid little attention to marital and other conflicts involved in Korean immigrant families. Instead, they have exaggerated what is seen on the surface—the work ethic, cohesion, and adaptability of immigrant families. The husband and the wife working together in a family business and high school students studying at home during their parents' absence make for an ideal image of a cohesive, upwardly mobile family. Thus, the *New York Times* and other mainstream media have featured stories of several Korean immigrant families, similar to the Kims introduced above, in an extremely positive manner.

Social scientists have not paid much attention to immigrant families, either. Researchers interested in immigrants have generally focused on the adjustments of individuals, particularly the economic adjustments of male immigrants, and the formation of immigrant communities. Of the more than one hundred monographs and edited books on contemporary immigrant groups published over the last two decades, only two focus exclusively on ethnic families (McAdoo 1993; Mindel et al. 1988), and only a few devote one or more separate chapters specifically to family adjustments (Caplan et al. 1989; Gold 1995; Hondagneu-Sotelo 1994; Kibria 1993; B. Kim 1978; Yu et al. 1982).

The vast majority of post-1965 immigrants have come from non-European, Third World countries, particularly from Asia, Latin America, and the Caribbean (Rumbaut 1994; Portes and Rumbaut 1990), where family systems are markedly different from American families. Not surprisingly, new immigrant groups experience enormous changes in family life, especially in women's economic roles, marital relations, and relations between parents and children, perhaps more significant changes than those experienced by earlier European immigrant groups.

One major change is that married women are more likely to work outside the home in the United States than in their home countries (Foner 1986; Perez 1986; Min 1992a; Pessar 1987; Sluzki 1979). However, researchers have shown that the increased participation in the labor force has not resulted in significant changes in immigrant women's—or their husbands'—gender role behaviors in the family (Ferre 1979; Foner 1986; A. Kim 1996; Kim and Hurh 1988; Kibria 1993; Liu et al. 1979; Min 1992a, 1995a, 1997a; Sluzki 1979). As a result, most immigrant wives suffer from overwork both inside and outside the home, and their expanded economic role has not liberated them from the chains of traditional patriarchy. In fact, the increase in immigrant women's economic role and changes in their role expectations often lead to marital conflicts and tensions as wives challenge the traditional authority of their husbands (Agbayani-Siewert 1991; Kibria 1993; Min 1995a; Sluzki 1979).

Parent–child relations also undergo significant changes when people move to this country. Of course, contemporary American families have a high level of parent–child conflict. But generational conflicts are exacerbated in immigrant families by enormous cultural differences between parents and their children. Immigrant parents usually speak their native languages and follow traditional customs at home, while their American-born children learn the English language and American customs from teachers, the mass media, and their American peers. Parents—fathers, in particular—exercise much greater authority over their children in Asian and Latin American countries than is accepted in the United States. However, in this country authoritarian child rearing practices are not acceptable to second- and 1.5-generation (those who were born in a foreign country but who immigrated at early ages) children who have been exposed to a much more liberal social and educational environment here. Thus, social workers and researchers report high levels of conflict and tension in parent–child relations in contemporary immigrant families (Agbayani-Siewert and Revilla 1995; Gold 1992: 86–87; Min 1995a; Sewell-Cocker et al. 1985; Sluzki 1979; Sung 1987: 183–184; Anderson and Thrasher 1988; Yu 1985: 56–58). Many immigrant parents feel stressed and frustrated over the loss of authority and control over their children.

THE FOCUS OF THE BOOK

This book is an in-depth study of the way the migration of Koreans to the United States has altered their traditional family system based on Confucianism. It focuses on changes in gender roles and marital relations; it also discusses the ways in which Korean immigrant parents socialize their children, as well as the adjustments of the elderly and the nature of transnational families and kin ties.

Traditionally, the U.S. media and researchers have depicted Asian immigrants as maintaining strong family ties and emphasized the harmony between husband and wife and parents and children. What is often stressed is that cultural mechanisms—strong family ties—have facilitated Asian immigrants' socioeconomic adjustments. In reaction to this emphasis on culture, a number of researchers have recently tried to examine Asian American families using a structural approach (Chow 1995; Glenn 1983, 1986; Glenn and Parrenas 1995; Kibria 1993; Wong 1988). For example, Glenn (1983: 35) has focused on the "changing structure of Chinese American families resulting from the interplay between shifting institutional constraints and the efforts of Chinese Americans to maintain family life in the face of these restrictions." In her ethnographic study of Vietnamese immigrant families, Kibria (1993: 22) has argued that "immigrant families must be studied in relation to the external structural conditions encountered by immigrants in the host society." Following a structural approach, researchers have recently paid more attention to marital and generational conflicts in Asian immigrant families than to cooperation and harmony.

In line with this newly emerging orientation, this book examines the effects of structural factors on Korean immigrant families. In particular, it explains how Korean immigrants' economic structures—namely concentration in small, family businesses—have modified their family relations. The prevalence of small family and ethnic businesses in the Korean community has increased Korean immigrant women's economic role, which, in turn, has led to a series of important consequences for the women themselves as well as their families. Because both partners often work long hours in the family store, child socialization patterns and parent–child relations are affected. The sudden increase in Korean immigrant wives' economic role without significant changes in their husbands' gender role attitudes—combined with both partners' long working hours—has led to marital conflicts and stress. Language barriers and cultural differences between Korean immigrant parents and their Americanized children have also created serious intergenerational conflicts and tensions in most Korean immigrant families. In view of these conflicts, the emphasis on family ties and harmony among Asian immigrant families by the mainstream media severely distorts reality.

Technological advances—another structural factor— have made possible Korean transnational families and transnational kin ties. Social scientists have recently tried to capture many features of the emerging reality of transnational linkages and connections (Abelmann and Lie 1995; Basch et al. 1994; Kearney 1994; Lessinger 1995: 87–95; Rodriguez 1994; Glick Schiller et al. 1992; Sutton 1987). With modern air transportation and telecommunications, Korean immigrants can maintain close contacts with kin members through regular visits and frequent long-distance telephone calls. Technological improvements have thus allowed Korean immigrants to maintain transnational families, with some family members living in the United States and others in South Korea.

By emphasizing the effects of structural conditions, I do not mean to ignore the role of Korean cultural traditions in shaping immigrant families. If earlier researchers put a one-sided emphasis on the role of family ties and values in facilitating Asian immigrants' adjustments, some revisionist critics of the cultural approach have failed to recognize the powerful influence of conservative family ideologies from the home country. Korean immigrants have brought with them a Confucian family ideology that emphasizes family/kin ties, filial piety, children's education, and an extreme form of patriarchy (Nivison and Wright 1959; Park and Cho 1994). As will be shown in chapter 2, Korean immigrants' economic segregation as well as their religious participation in ethnic congregations have helped them maintain Korean cultural traditions, including the Confucian family ideology. This family ideology has wide-ranging effects, particularly on Korean immigrants' child socialization patterns and marital relations. Not all Korean immigrants accept the family hierarchy prescribed by the Confucian ideology to the same degree. Indeed, it is Americanized Korean children's challenge of authoritarian Korean child socialization techniques and Korean wives' attempt to moderate the traditional patriarchal system, along with Korean men's resistance to change, that have created generational and marital conflicts.

ETHNOGRAPHIC RESEARCH

This book uses ethnographic research to document the struggles, conflicts, and tensions in Korean immigrant families. As a Korean immigrant, I have an insider's knowledge of my own and other Korean immigrant families. My personal family experiences, my casual observations of other Korean families, my informal discussions with Korean school teachers and social workers and my reading of Korean ethnic newspaper articles have sensitized me to the pervasiveness and seriousness of conflicts and tensions in Korean immigrant families.

I have also used thirty intensive, personal interviews and twenty telephone interviews with Koreans in New York—including immigrant men, women, children, and elderly persons. Three of the women and one student interviewed were people who contacted me for counseling. The others were located by myself, my wife, children, friends, and community social workers. All the men and women, with the exception of four elderly persons and a divorced woman, were married and represented the cross-section of Korean immigrants in term of age, educational level, occupational type, and length of residence in this country. Qualitative data based on tape-recorded personal interviews are useful in documenting dynamics of family relations (LaRossa 1985; Rubin 1976, 1983). My unstructured personal and telephone interviews with Korean immigrants have provided the major data for the family stories introduced throughout the book.

I conducted all but four interviews, using a loosely structured, open-ended questionnaire, adjusting questions to fit special characteristics of each respondent. Most personal interviews lasted one hour and were conducted using tape-recorders either at the respondent's home, store, office, or in my office. The interviews were conducted between June 1996 and February 1997. In most cases, I have used pseudonyms to protect the privacy of the interviewees. In some cases, I have also altered the details of the interview slightly so that the interviewee is not identified by those who know them personally.

In order to better understand Korean immigrant families in New York, I also interviewed a dozen staff members who work for ethnic organizations that provide various services for these families as I was writing this book. They include after-school centers, churches, family counseling centers, and elderly centers. In most cases, I visited the ethnic organizations and made first-hand observations of their activities and personally interviewed the staff members. In other cases, I conducted the interviews by telephone.

Finally, I have used census and survey data to provide statistical information about Korean immigrant families. Although qualitative data are important for capturing the complex dynamics of family life, it is dangerous to generalize from participant observations and interviews with a few individual cases. We need quantitative data on the characteristics of the group. For example, a discussion of the increased economic role and role strains of Korean immigrant women requires quantitative data showing that most Korean immigrant wives participate in the labor force while a small proportion of wives in South Korea do so. In addition to drawing on census reports and surveys by other researchers, I have used data from five surveys of Koreans in New York that I conducted between 1988 and 1996.

My 1988 survey was based on 297 telephone interviews with a randomly selected sample of Korean married women in New York City and focused on changes in Korean immigrant women's gender roles (see Min 1992a for a discussion of data collection techniques). My 1989 survey was based on responses to a questionnaire by about 460 Korean high school students, not randomly selected, in New York; the survey looked at Korean high school students' ethnic attachment, home and school lives, and educational and occupational plans. In the 1991 survey, I examined parent–child relations in Korean immigrant families, using 65 sets of responses to a questionnaire by a mother and a child from each family (see Min 1995b for a discussion of data collection techniques of the 1991 survey). The 1993 survey was based on administration of a questionnaire to, or personal interviews with, 152 Korean elderly persons (not randomly selected) in New York. It examined various aspects of adjustments of elderly Korean immigrants. The 1996 survey was based on telephone interviews with 99 randomly selected Korean immigrants in Queens, New York City. It focused on ethnic attachments of Korean, Chinese, and Indian immigrants. These five data sets provide information about the structure of Korean immigrant families as well as about the nature of family relations.

2

The Korean Community in New York

Although Korean immigration has a history of nearly one hundred years, the vast majority of pre-1965 Korean immigrants were concentrated in Hawaii and the West Coast states, particularly California. Over the last thirty years, a large proportion of Korean immigrants have flocked to New York City and several suburban counties surrounding the city, including Suffolk, Nassau, Bergen, and Westchester Counties. As a result, the New York–New Jersey area has become the home to about 150,000 Koreans, making it the second largest Korean population center in this country, following Southern California. Residentially, Koreans in New York are heavily concentrated in Flushing, establishing another Koreatown in the downtown Flushing area. Economically, they have a near monopoly in produce retail, dry cleaning, and several other types of small businesses. Socially, Koreans in New York maintain strong ethnic networks, represented by churches, ethnic media, and alumni associations.

CONTEMPORARY MIGRATION

Korean migration to the United States dates from the beginning of this century, when about 7,200 Korean laborers came to Hawaii between 1903 and 1905 to work on the sugar plantations there (Patterson 1987). Although Hawaiian plantation owners needed more Korean workers, in 1905 the Japanese government forced the Korean government to stop sending more laborers to Hawaii. In that year, Korea had become Japan's protectorate as a result of Japan's victory in the Russo-Japanese War, giving Japan the ability to influence Korean government policy.

Before U.S. legislation in the early 1920s barred Korean immigration completely, approximately 2,000 additional Koreans moved to Hawaii and the West Coast states. In the period between 1906 and 1924, the vast majority of Korean immigrants were "picture brides" of the pioneer immigrants in Hawaii or political refugees engaged in the anti-Japanese movement in Korea. Although the earlier Korean labor migrants on the West Coast intended to go back to Korea when they made enough money, most of them and their picture brides remained in the United States permanently. However, the majority of political refugees went back to their home country when Korea became independent of Japanese colonization in 1945.

As a result of the Korean War in 1950, the United States became heavily involved in South Korea as a close military, political, and economic ally. The linkages between the two countries helped to stimulate a new wave of immigration to the United States. About 15,000 Koreans moved to the United States between 1950 and 1964. Most were Korean orphans who had been adopted by American citizens, or Korean women who had married U.S. servicemen stationed in South Korea. A growing number of Korean children adopted by American citizens and internationally married Korean women left for the United States in the 1970s and 1980s.

Altogether fewer than 50,000 Koreans lived in the United States in 1960. The number of Korean immigrants accelerated with the passage of the 1965 Immigration Act. Annual Korean immigration, only a few thousands in the 1960s, rapidly increased in the early 1970s. More than 30,000 Koreans immigrated to the United States annually between 1976 and 1990, constituting the third largest immigrant group during the period, following Mexicans and Filipinos.

As economic migrants, Koreans were largely motivated to come to the United States by the prospect of obtaining a higher standard of living than in their home country. Many Koreans also moved to give their children better opportunities for education, particularly for college education (Kim and Min 1992; Min 1995a; Yoon 1993). By the 1990s, when South Korea had achieved great economic prosperity, better educational opportunities may well have been more important than pure economic motives for many Korean immigrants. Of continued importance, too, are the military, political, and economic linkages between the United States and South Korea and the consequent American cultural influence in South Korea.

Peaking in 1987, when nearly 36,000 Koreans came to the United States, Korean immigration has gradually decreased to approximately 16,000 in 1994. This recent reduction is a result of great improvements in economic and political conditions in South Korea and better information there about the difficulties that most Korean immigrants have had in the United States. In the 1970s, when there was a huge gap in living standards between the United States and South Korea, the vast majority of Korean immigrants were from the middle class and upper-middle class. However, few middle-class Koreans are now motivated to emigrate from South Korea, where per capita income reached the $10,000 mark in 1995. In fact, the expanding South Korean economy has recently attracted many Koreans who completed their professional education in the United States, including second-generation Korean Americans. Politically, in 1987 a civilian government based on a popular election replaced the military government that had pushed many Korean intellectuals out of the country. Also, the fear of another war in the Korean peninsula has been substantially reduced as North Korea is struggling for survival in the wake of the breakdown of the former Soviet Union and other communist governments.

The influx of Korean immigrants over the last quarter century has led to an enormous growth in the Korean population here. The 1990 census counted approximately 800,000 Koreans in the United States, with the U.S. born making up

28 percent. Considering a significant underestimation by the 1990 census and increases since then, the population of Korean ancestry is likely to be approximately 1.2 million as of 1996. In 1990, the Korean population accounted for 12 percent of approximately 7.3 million Asian Americans, but the proportion is likely to be lower in the future. Korean immigration has been decreasing, while the immigration flow from other Asian countries has greatly increased in the 1990s.

Recent Korean immigrants generally represent the middle-class strata of the Korean population. The 1990 census indicated that 34 percent of Korean immigrants who were twenty-five or older had completed four years of college and that 80 percent had completed high school (U.S. Bureau of the Census 1993b: 84). In contrast, 20 percent of the U.S. population had received a college education and 75 percent had completed high school (U.S. Bureau of the Census 1993b: 72). Moreover, recent Korean immigrants far surpass the educational level of the general population in Korea. The 1990 Korean census indicated that only 14 percent of Korean adults had completed four years of college education (Korean Women's Development Institute 1994: 70).

Consistent with their high educational level, most recent Korean immigrants held professional and white-collar jobs before they emigrated. Nearly half of the Korean respondents in a Chicago study indicated that their pre-immigrant occupations had been professional, administrative, managerial, or technical, whereas only 7 percent said they had held blue-collar jobs in Korea (Hurh and Kim 1988). A survey of Korean immigrants in the Los Angeles-Orange County area showed similarly high pre-immigrant occupational backgrounds. Fifty-four percent of the respondents who were working in Korea just before they left had held professional, administrative, executive, and managerial jobs, and only 4 percent had been employed in blue-collar occupations (Min 1989).

Recent Korean immigrants are also characterized by their urban background. Approximately 1,800 prospective Korean immigrants were interviewed in 1986 at the U.S. Consulate in Seoul at the time of their visa interview. Though only a quarter of the entire Korean population lives in the capital city, more than half of the respondents in this predeparture survey reported that they resided in Seoul (Park et al. 1990: 31). The survey also indicated that more than three-fourths lived in the five largest cities in Korea at the time of their interview. While many residents in Seoul and other large Korean cities originally came from rural areas, they quickly became familiar with the Korean urban life style before departing for the United States.

Recent Korean immigrants are also a select group in terms of their religious background. Although only about 25 percent of all Koreans are affiliated with Christian churches in South Korea (Park and Cho 1994), most Korean immigrants practiced Christianity in Korea. For example, in a survey of a 1986 group of Korean immigrants conducted in Seoul (Park et al. 1990: 60), 54 percent of the respondents reported that they were affiliated with Protestant (41.6%) or Catholic (12.3%) churches. Another survey, conducted in Chicago, indicated that 53 percent of Korean immigrants had been Christians in Korea (Hurh and Kim 1990). Korean immigrants have been drawn largely from the urban, middle-class segment of the Korean population, in which Christianity is practiced heavily. This contributes to a disproportionate representation of Christians among Korean immigrants. Also, Korean Christians are more likely than Buddhists, Confucians, or those not affiliated with a religion to move to the United States where it is easier to practice their religion.

SETTLEMENT IN NEW YORK

In the pre-1965 era, Koreans were heavily concentrated in the West Coast and almost invisible in New York. The number of Koreans was so small in 1960 that the census did not classify them separately. An informal source indicates that there then were no more than 400 Koreans in New York and that the majority were Korean students who planned to return to Korea after completion of their study (The Korean Association of New York 1985: 54).

However, a large proportion of post-1965 Korean immigrants settled in New York City and several suburban counties surrounding the city, including Bergen, Westchester, and Suffolk Counties. In 1990, 12 percent of all Korean Americans were settled in New York state, a substantial increase from 9.6 percent in 1980. Another 5 percent of Korean Americans were settled in New Jersey, which marked a 200 percent growth rate in the Korean population between 1980 and 1990. Together, the New York–New Jersey metropolitan area is home to approximately 150,000 Korean Americans. In the 1960s, the New York–New Jersey area, with an expanding medical industry, needed many medical professionals. The demand for medical professionals in the area attracted many Korean and other Asian (Indian and Filipino in particular) medical professionals immediately after the passage of the Immigration Act of 1965 (I. Kim 1981: 155–156; Rosenthal 1995). By the early 1980s, many Korean medical and other occupational immigrants in New York had become naturalized citizens so that they were able to invite their relatives for permanent residence.

While Manhattan was the center of the Korean community in New York before 1965, Queens has attracted the most post-1965 Korean immigrants; 70 percent of the city's Korean population lives in the borough of Queens. Koreans in Queens are heavily concentrated in Flushing, which has gone through a radical ethnic change in the last two decades from a predominantly white area to a multiethnic community. Queens in general and Flushing in particular have attracted many Chinese, Indian, and other Asian immigrants, including Koreans, in the post-1965 era. In 1990, nearly a quarter of the population in Community District 7, which combines Flushing, Whitestone, and College Point, was composed of Asian and Pacific Islander Americans. The share of the Asian population in the district as of 1996 is likely to be over 30 percent. In 1996, two Koreans and a Chinese were elected as members of the nine-member school board in the 25th School District encompassing Flushing, Whitestone, and College Point.

Since the early 1980s, Koreatown has been in formation in downtown Flushing. Flushing Koreatown covers approximately twenty blocks east of downtown Flushing where Koreans are heavily clustered. Although not comparable to

Koreatown in Los Angeles, Flushing Koreatown has all the elements of a traditional ethnic neighborhood. In addition to being New York City Koreans' residential center, it has hundreds of Korean stores with Korean language signs. Korean businesses in Flushing Koreatown include restaurants, grocery stores, barber shops, beauty salons, bakeries, dental/medical offices, law offices, accounting firms, insurance, real estate and travel agencies. These businesses depend almost entirely on Korean customers. Since Korean businesses in Flushing are heavily concentrated on Union Street between Northern Boulevard and 38th Avenue, the area is called the Union Korean Business District ("Union Hanin Sanga"). Korean restaurants in the Flushing area are in such intense competition that prices for Korean food there are lower than in Seoul.

Like other ethnic neighborhoods, Flushing Koreatown is New York Koreans' social and cultural center as well. Two dozen Korean social service agencies are located there. They include the Korean YMCA, YWCA, the Korean Youth Service Center, the Korean Family Counseling Center, the Korean Senior Citizens Society, the Korean Small Business Service Center, and the Korean Association of Flushing. Approximately seventy Korean Christian congregations have been established in the Flushing area. Every week, several Korean ethnic meetings are held at Korean offices and Korean restaurants in Flushing. Also, many Korean families who live outside as well as in Flushing hold various ceremonies at Koreatown restaurants. Flushing Koreatown has dozens of Korean lodging houses that provide visitors from Korea with rooms and food.

Koreans in Bergen County are most visible in the Fort Lee downtown area. As of November 1996, about 3,500 Korean students were enrolled in four elementary, one junior, and one senior high school in Fort Lee, accounting for 30 percent of the area's students (*The Sae Gae Times*, 1996b). Approximately one hundred Korean businesses with Korean language signs are clustered in a Fort Lee downtown area. Also, there are a Korean language school and several other Korean ethnic organizations in the Fort Lee area. Koreans consider the Fort Lee Korean enclave New York's "suburban

Koreatown" comparable to the Monterey Park Chinatown in Los Angeles. Palisades, not far from Fort Lee, also has attracted a large number of Koreans during recent years. Many Korean restaurants, drinking places, and other ethnic stores catering to Korean customers have mushroomed in the Palisades downtown area. They usually display large Korean language signs and use English signs too small for American residents to read. The non-Korean residents in Palisades and neighboring cities have shown their resentment against Koreans' failure to use English signs and their late night commercial activities by initiating and supporting new ordinances requiring businesses to have English signs as large as native language signs and to close at midnight.

CONCENTRATION IN SMALL BUSINESSES

American citizens in Los Angeles, New York, and other major cities cannot pass their downtown areas without encountering Korean-owned stores. Not only African American residents but also the American public in general are familiar with Koreans' commercial activities in many African American neighborhoods, as the mainstream media have publicized conflicts between Korean merchants and African American customers. The visibility of Korean-owned stores and the media publicity of Korean–African American conflicts have led the American public to perceive Korean immigrants as a trading minority.

Census and survey data show that the perception of Korean immigrants as highly entrepreneurial is based on reality. For example, 1990 census data indicate that 34.5 percent of foreign-born Koreans in Los Angeles were self-employed (Light and Roach 1996). Korean immigrants showed the highest self-employment rate among all minority and immigrant groups in Los Angeles. Census data undercount the self-employment rate of Koreans as well as of the general population. My 1986 survey showed that 45 percent of Korean immigrants in Los Angeles and Orange Counties were self-employed (Min 1996: 48). A survey conducted in New York City revealed an even higher self-employment rate—over 50 percent (Min 1996: 48). Since another 30 percent of Korean immigrants work for Korean-owned businesses, the vast majority of the Korean work force is segregated in the Korean subeconomy either as business owners or as employees of co-ethnic businesses. The economic segregation of Korean immigrants has important implications for their family lives as well as for their intergroup relations and community structure.

Researchers on immigrant and ethnic entrepreneurship agree that disadvantages in gaining employment in the general labor market push immigrants and minority members to self-employment in small business, but that only those groups with ethnic and class resources for entrepreneurship develop a high level of ethnic business (Light and Rosenstein 1995, Chapter 5; Min 1987; Waldinger et al 1990). Korean immigrants fit this picture. Although they are, as a group, highly educated, with many Korean immigrant men having college degrees, they come to America with distinct labor market disadvantages, namely a lack of fluency in English and unfamiliarity with American customs. Indian and Filipino professional immigrants who spoke English in their home countries and were more exposed to Western educational systems are more successful than Korean professional immigrants in being able to practice their occupations in this country (Min 1986–87). Still, Koreans' labor market disadvantages alone cannot explain their high self-employment rate. Their economic advantages in the form of business capital and managerial experience and their strong ethnic ties (to be discussed later in this chapter) help them establish and operate businesses. Although many immigrants from mainland China and many Vietnamese refugees are motivated to start small businesses that involve long hours of work, they do not have the kinds of resources that Koreans bring with them.

Because Korean immigrants in the 1970s came to the United States neither expecting to, nor prepared to, start their own businesses, it took them several years before they established businesses. More recently, this has changed. Korean immigrants now come here better prepared to set up businesses. For one thing, they are well informed in Korea that self-employment in small business is the only alternative for most Korean immigrants. In fact, a survey of prospective Korean immigrants conducted in Seoul in 1986 showed that recent Korean immigrants usually expect to run a small business in the United States (Park et al 1990: 86). Recent immigrants also often bring enough money with them to establish their own businesses. Once they arrive here, they easily acquire business information and training by working in Korean-owned enterprises. For example, Byung Ho Choi, who came to Flushing in June 1994, started his produce retail business within six months of immigration. Although his brother, an accountant, lived in Los Angeles, he chose to come to Flushing because he could easily get business training and information from a produce retail store run by his high school friend. After working five months at his friend's store, he bought a produce store in Woodside from a Korean owner for $180,000. He used a downpayment of $60,000— $45,000 from his condominium sale in Seoul and $15,000 from a private loan from his high school friend.

MAJOR KOREAN BUSINESSES IN NEW YORK

Korean immigrants' commercial activities in New York are limited to several types of labor-intensive small businesses, most of which are not attractive to native-born Americans. Green groceries are probably the best-known Korean business in New York. Korean immigrants are able to start produce stores with small amounts of money, since the cash turnaround is very quick. They are ready to work long hours and have access to the cheap labor needed to operate produce stores. Many Koreans bought produce stores from retiring Jewish and Italian American owners in Queens and Manhattan beginning in the 1970s. In the 1980s, Koreans opened up produce stores in nearly every neighborhood in New York City, including low-income African American neighborhoods. More Korean produce stores are located in low-income African American neighborhoods than in white middle-class areas. Several Korean-owned produce stores in Harlem, Jamaica and Brooklyn's Flatbush area were the targets of long-term boycotts. By now there are approximately 2,000 Korean-owned produce stores in New York, controlling about 60 percent of independent produce stores in the city.

Trade businesses dealing in wigs, handbags, clothing, and other fashion items make up another major type of Korean business in New York. Most of the merchandise of this sort is imported from South Korea and other Asian countries. Korean immigrants have advantages in establishing and operating retail stores dealing in Asian-imported items in terms of getting credit and business information. The New York Korean community has over 500 Korean importers who distribute Asian-imported manufactured goods largely to Korean wholesalers and retailers all over the country (Min 1996: 55–56).

About 400 Korean import businesses in New York are located in Manhattan's Broadway Korean Business District, a rectangular, ten-block area from 24th Street to 34th Street between Fifth and Sixth Avenues. The intersection of 32nd Street and Broadway is considered its center. Also located in this Broadway area are a number of Korean restaurants, Korean professional businesses such as law and accounting firms, travel agencies, and gift shops that serve mainly Korean wholesalers and importers. There is also one Korean-owned motel in this district, mainly serving tourists from Korea and other parts of the United States. The Korean Businessmen's Association, the association of Korean importers in the Broadway Korean Business District, lobbied the New York City government to post a Koreatown sign in the area. As a result, in October 1995, the city named the district "Koreatown" and posted official signs at the intersection between 32nd Street and Broadway.

Dry cleaning service is another major Korean business in New York, as well as in other Korean communities. There are approximately 1,500 Korean-owned dry cleaners in New York. Korean immigrants are attracted to the dry cleaning business partly because it is suitable as a family business involving the husband and the wife. Korean-owned dry cleaning shops are usually located in white, middle-class neighborhoods. Like other small businesses in New York, the dry cleaning industry was controlled by Jewish and Italian Americans before the 1970s. In that decade, Koreans in New York began to buy dry cleaning stores from these white ethnics in predominantly white middle-class areas. Since 1980s, many Koreans have bought or newly opened dry cleaning stores all over the city.

Koreans in New York also control the nail salon business. They concentrate in the manicure business for the same reasons as earlier immigrants: the unimportance of language skills, the small amount of start-up capital necessary, and the lack of required professional skills. Koreans can rent the second, or basement, floor of a building to open a nail salon. Korean women initially began nail salons, but Korean men have entered this business in large numbers over the last several years, as the business has been touted as a source of profit for Korean immigrants. A Korean male owner often has several nail salons and hires Korean women as managers to run the business. As the number of Korean-owned nail salons rose dramatically during the 1980s, the price for a manicure in New York City fell to such an extent that low-income women can now afford to have the service.

TIGHT COMMUNITY ORGANIZATION

If Korean immigrants stand out because of their concentration in small business, their community is also noteworthy on account of its tight organization. In the Korean community, there are far more ethnic organizations in proportion to population size than in any other Asian ethnic community. The Korean community in the New York metropolitan area has more ethnic associations than either the Chinese or the Indian community, although its population is only about 30 percent of the Chinese population and 70 percent of the Indian population. In a survey conducted in Queens, New York in 1996, 82 percent of Korean immigrants were affiliated with one or more ethnic organization in comparison to 18 percent of the Chinese and 54 percent of the Indian immigrants.

As previously noted, over half of Korean immigrants were affiliated with a Protestant or Catholic church in Korea. Even Korean immigrants who were Buddhists or not affiliated with any religion in Korea often attend a Korean church in the United States for fellowship and other practical purposes (Min 1992b). Survey studies conducted in major Korean communities indicate that more than 70 percent of Korean immigrants attend a Korean church at least once a week (Hurh and Kim 1990; Min 1989; Min and Chen 1997). Historically, ethnic churches have played a role in sustaining ethnicity for new immigrant groups (Fenton 1988; Tomasi and Engel 1970: 186; Warner and Srole 1945: 160). The active participation of Korean immigrants in Korean churches helps them maintain their regular social interactions (Min 1992b). In fact, Korean immigrants are more actively involved in ethnic networks than Chinese or Indian immigrants mainly because the vast majority of them regularly participate in ethnic churches. Korean immigrant churches usually have an hour-long fellowship after the service, during which members exchange greetings and enjoy talks with refreshments offered. Many Korean churches in New York provide a full lunch after the Sunday service. Churches also help Korean immigrants maintain their cultural traditions by providing Korean language programs for children and by celebrating traditional Korean holidays with Korean foods (Min 1992b).

Korean immigrants are a homogeneous group in term of culture, language, and historical experiences. Group homogeneity and lack of diversity provide the cultural basis for Korean ethnic identity and solidarity (Min 1991). Korean immigrants' group homogeneity may be even more important for their ethnic attachment than Korean religious congregations themselves. Indeed, because of their group homogeneity, the vast majority of Korean immigrants are drawn to Korean congregations. Although 85 percent of Filipino immigrants are Catholics, most participate in American Catholic congregations rather than Filipino ethnic congregations (Pido 1986). It seems that Filipino immigrants, marked by ingroup diversity and internal divisions, consider participation in an ethnic congregation far less important than Korean immigrants do.

Korean immigrants speak a single language. This monolingual background gives Korean immigrants a big advantage over other multilingual groups, such as Indians and Filipinos, in maintaining ethnic attachment. Korean immigrants, all of whom can speak, read, and write the Korean language fluently, depend mainly on the Korean-language ethnic media—dailies, TV, and radio programs—for news, information, and leisure activities. Their almost exclusive dependence on the ethnic media, in turn, has strengthened their ties to the ethnic community and the home country. With advances in technology and communication, immigrants in New York hear same-day news broadcasts from Korea, watch new Korean movies and TV programs on videotapes, and can travel by air to Korea within fifteen hours. The distance between Seoul and American cities has become much shorter. The Korean ethnic media are extremely influential in maintaining Korean cultural traditions and identity, especially because Koreans use only one language. In contrast, since Indian and Filipino immigrants use several dialects, English is used in their ethnic media.

Research has shown that people who work in the ethnic economy are more actively involved in ethnic networks than those in the general economy (Bonacich and Modell 1980; Fugita and O'Brien 1991; Reitz 1980). Thus, immigrant and minority groups that have developed an extensive ethnic economy exhibit stronger ethnic attachment than those groups with fewer members working in ethnic businesses. The vast majority of Korean immigrant workers are in the Korean ethnic economy, either as business owners or as employees of Korean-owned businesses. The segregation of Korean immigrants at the workplace facilitates the preservation of their Korean cultural traditions and social interactions with co-ethnics (Min 1991), although it hinders their assimilation into American society. Most Korean immigrants work with family members, or at least co-ethnics, speaking the Korean language and practicing Korean customs during work hours. Koreans segregated at the workplace have little opportunity to make friends with non-Korean residents. Indeed, during off-duty hours, they maintain social interactions mainly with co-ethnics.

Korean immigrants' concentration in small business has also strengthened their ethnic solidarity. As noted, many Korean immigrants engage in middleman businesses such as grocery, green grocery, and liquor stores, that connect large corporations with low-income minority customers. Historically, middleman merchants suffered boycotts, riots, and other forms of hostility (Turner and Bonacich 1980; Eitzen 1971; Zenner 1991). Korean merchants in African American neighborhoods have experienced various forms of rejection and hostility (Min 1996).The victimization of Korean merchants due to their middleman economic role climaxed in the 1992 Los Angeles riots during which 2,300 Korean-owned stores in South Central Los Angeles and Koreatown were destroyed. Hostility against Korean merchants in African American neighborhoods, in turn, has contributed to Korean ethnic solidarity. For example, during the 1990–91 boycott of two Korea stores in New York, many Koreans as

Most produce stores in low-income, African American neighborhoods in New York City are owned by Korean immigrants. Several of them became targets of long-term boycotts. This is one of the stores in Jamaica, Queens. Photo taken by the author.

well as Korean merchants in the city participated in fund-raising campaigns, collecting approximately $150,000 to help the "victims of African American racism against Koreans." Also, dissatisfied with Mayor David Dinkin's "lukewarm" effort to terminate the boycott, the Korean community organized a demonstration in front of City Hall that drew approximately 7,000 Koreans.

Economic interests bring Koreans into conflict with white suppliers and white landlords, and with government agencies that regulate small businesses. Establishing trade associations, Koreans have used collective strategies to protect their economic interests from these powerful forces. For example, since the early 1970s the Korean Produce Association of New York has organized several boycotts of white wholesalers to try to put an end to discriminatory practices and to improve overrall services to Korean merchants. The Korean Small Business Service Center and several other Korean trade associations in New York have been active in lobbying administrators and politicians to moderate regulations of small businesses. In their efforts to resolve business-related intergroup conflicts and negotiate with government agencies to protect their economic interests, Korean trade associations and business leaders have exercised a great deal of influence and power in the Korean community.In terms of membership, budget, and organizational activities, Korean trade associations are far more powerful than Korean professional associations (Min 1996).

3

Confucianism and the Korean Family System

Confucianism, which originated in China, was introduced to Korea in the fourth century. It began to have a powerful cultural influence in Korea during the Yi dynasty (1392–1910) when the government adopted Confucianism as a social, political, and economic philosophy (Pak 1983; Park and Cho 1994). The Confucian ideology was most influential in Korea before Christian religions were adopted in the beginning of the twentieth century. Even now, Confucian values that emphasize filial piety, family/kin ties, the patriarchal family order, and children's education still have a powerful effect on the behaviors and attitudes of all Koreans, whether they are Catholics, Protestants, Buddhists, or atheists. Indeed, it is impossible to understand Korean traditional culture in general and the family system in particular, without understanding the influence of Chinese Confucianism.

Concerned mainly with life in this world rather than in the other world, Confucius provided several important principles to serve as a guide for behavior and harmonious social relations. Five categories of interpersonal relations form the basis of his teachings concerning the duties and obligations of each individual. These relations are between parents and children, king and people, husband and wife, older (brother) and younger (brother), and friends. The significance of

Confucianism for the Korean family system is clear as three of these five cardinal relations involve the family. In fact, no other religion or ideology puts more emphasis on the family as the fundamental unit of society than Confucianism. For this reason, Confucianism is considered a familial religion.

FILIAL PIETY

Confucius viewed establishing and maintaining good order in the family as the primary means of safeguarding social security and stability. In order to establish and maintain order in the family, he envisioned a hierarchical organization of family that justified children's loyalty, respect, and devotion to their parents, and a wife's subordination to her husband. The phrase "filial piety" characterizes the emphasis on children's obligations and devotion to parents. Children were required not only to pay the highest respect to parents throughout their lives but also to fulfill important obligations to them. The eldest son was supposed to live with his parents after marriage, providing them with financial support and care. Moreover, filial piety was extended after the death of a parent in the form of ancestor worship. Sons observed ritual mourning for three years after a parent died, and younger generations of sons showed worshipful veneration to their ancestors in the three preceding generations.

Although high levels of urbanization and industrialization have led to great changes in the traditional family system, filial piety, or *hyodo*, is still considered one of the cardinal virtues in contemporary Korean society. The government, school, and community encourage people to practice *hyodo* by rewarding those who are exceptional in showing loyalty, respect, and devotion to their parents and by punishing those who deviate far from the norm. The norm of filial piety has given parents, especially fathers, authority and control over their children. Children are not supposed to talk back to parents even when parents are wrong. To show their respect and politeness, children use different words (*jaundae mal*) and behaviors when interacting with parents and elderly persons than when interacting with their friends. Whenever giving something to a parent or an adult, they use both hands.

Although the vast majority of households in South Korea are nuclear families, elderly parents usually live with their eldest married son. They receive financial support and health care from children, particularly from the cohabiting eldest son, as government programs for support and care of elderly persons are almost non-existent. According to the 1990 Korean census, 80 percent of elderly persons in South Korea reside with their children, 66 percent with their married children (Eu 1992). Eldest sons have disadvantages in finding marital partners because they are supposed to live with their elderly parents. When women start dating to select their marital partners, they first ask their partners whether they are eldest sons or not. Although the cohabiting eldest son is mainly responsible for the financial support and health care of his elderly parents, all his brothers and sisters share some responsibility. They often give their parents pocket money, buy air tickets for *hyodo kwankwang* (travel for filial piety), and donate money for their parents' birthday parties. In South Korea, children organize a big party for their parent's sixtieth birthday, spending a lot of money. It is not unusual for brothers and sisters to argue over who should contribute more money for the birthday party.

The Confucian ideology prescribes that filial obligations be perpetuated after the death of a parent through ritual ancestor worship. Although practiced in China and Japan, ancestor worship has had greater effects on Korean society (Janeli and Janeli 1982). Ancestor worship in traditional Korea required children to mourn for three years after the death of a parent. Domestic rites were performed annually for ancestors, with food and wine offered on their death dates (*chesa*) and important holidays (*cha'rye*), usually on New Year's Day and the Harvest Moon Festival (*Ch'usok*). Ancestor worship was based on the belief that the ancestors' souls would visit their descendants' homes to eat food offerings and that the failure to perform ancestral rituals would provoke a soul to punish descendants. Although the eldest son was usually responsible for offering the rites at his home and bore most of the expenses, all male agnatic descendants were responsible for commemorating a given ancestor. In addition to ritual services to his deceased parents, an eldest son assumed any ritual responsibilities his father had toward agnatic forebears within the three previous generations (Janeli and Janeli 1982: 99). In traditional Korean society, kin group members usually lived in the same village, partly for the convenience of performing these ancestral rituals.

In highly urbanized, contemporary Korean society, there are few kin-based villages, with kin group members usually living in different cities. But even today, many people in South Korea make an inter-city visit to their agnatic descendant's home for death-day and holiday rites.

PATRIARCHY

Confucian ideology accorded men the dominant position and thus helped to establish an extreme form of patriarchy in Korea. In traditional Korean society, the husband was considered the primary breadwinner and decision-maker in the family and exercised authority over his wife and children. The wife was expected to obey her husband, devotedly serving him and his kin, and to perpetuate her husband's lineage by bearing children. The wife was excluded from decision making in important family affairs, including her children's education. She was able to exercise some power and influence only through her son, who, according to the norm of filial piety, was supposed to obey his mother at least before his marriage. In traditional Korean society, women were not allowed to perform ancestral worship services for their own relatives. Widows were not allowed to remarry, whereas married men were allowed to take concubines.

High levels of industrialization and Westernization have led to many changes in the traditional family system in South Korea in recent years. However, there is no fundamental change in patriarchy and gender inequality based on Confucian ideology. Both traditional gender role expectations and employment discrimination discourage married women from participating in the labor market. The 1990 Korean census shows that only one-quarter of married women in urban areas participate in the labor force (Korean Bureau of Statistics 1993). Although many women work outside the home before they get married, once they marry, they usually quit their jobs, often involuntarily, to be *hyonmo yangch'o* (a wise mother and good wife). According to one survey conducted in 1985, over 80 percent of the women who had been employed prior to marriage quit their jobs upon marriage to concentrate in housework (B. Kim 1994: 246). Recently, the number of women graduating from college has increased. However, most college-educated women in South Korea become full-time housewives when they get married. In fact, many parents send their daughters to college to help them find desirable partners.

A strong double standard exists in Korea: a husband's extramarital affairs with single women are tacitly condoned, whereas a wife's extramarital affairs are heavily punished. Korean husbands still tend to view their wives primarily as housekeepers and mothers. Whether wives work outside the home or not, husbands are not much involved in traditional housework chores such as cooking, dishwashing, and cleaning (Cho 1994). Unless working wives have an elderly mother-in-law, a grown-up daughter, and/or a maid to help with housework, they are almost entirely responsible for housework chores. Not only Korean men but also women themselves accept traditional gender role attitudes. In a survey comparing American and Korean women, 82 percent of Korean women agreed with the statement, "Women should have only a family-oriented life, devoted to bringing up the children and looking after the husband," in contrast to only 19 percent of American women (B. Kim 1994).

The Korean notion of motherhood, deeply rooted in the Confucian ideology, emphasizes the role of mother's love and devotion in child care and child socialization. Most married women with a child in Korea cannot separate their identity from their child and/or husband. As I discuss in the next section, Korean women with school-age children spend much of their time and energy in organizing and supervising their children's extracurricular studies after school. Since women's success is measured largely on how well their children perform in school, most college-educated women give up their own careers to concentrate on their children's education. Those few women who maintain their careers suffer from triple burdens of paid work, housework, and child care.

Men in Korea, regardless of class background, usually work long hours at their jobs, many working until after seven in the evening. After work, they often meet with their friends for dinner and go drinking without giving their wives any notice. While men enjoy after-work hours socializing with their friends outside the home, their wives take care of the housework and the children, many waiting for their husbands until late at night to eat dinner together. Although fathers put pressure on their children to do well in school, most do not find time to help their children with homework. Housewives in Korea complain about their husbands spending little time at home in general and about their excessive drinking in particular. According to recent media reports, women's confinement to home where they do housework and take care of children and their lack of marital companionship cause serious psychological problems for many housewives.

The connections between patriarchy on the one hand and patrilineal kinship (descent through men on the father's side) and patrilocal residence (the married couple living with the husband's family) on the other are clearly discernible in contemporary Korean society. The tradition that the eldest married son or another married son live with elderly parents is still observed in Korea. A cohabiting daughter-in-law is mainly responsible for taking care of her husband's elderly parents. Those elderly Koreans without a son have difficulty getting financial and health care support, as there is almost no governmental program to help the elderly. By custom, a married daughter is not supposed to live with her own elderly parent even if the latter is sick. She can provide health care for the parent only informally by visiting his/her home. People in South Korea are anxious to have at least one son because this is similar to having a pension and medical insurance in the United States. According to the 1990 census, among children under ten, boys outnumber girls by 109 to 100 (Korean Women's Development Institute 1994: 38). This imbalance in favor of boys is presumed to have been caused by sex-specific abortions, which is an issue of great concern in contemporary Korean society.

The case of my own aunt and her daughter illustrates the difficulty that an elderly person with no son experiences in Korea. My aunt's only surviving child is a daughter. The daughter is married to a man who is an only son. My aunt, 68, has been sick for many years because of a traffic accident she was involved in fifteen years ago. But my cousin (her daughter) has lived with her healthy mother-in-law ever since she got married. Her mother-in-law could have lived with one of her two daughters, but the Korean custom did not allow for such an arrangement. My cousin has only been able to take care of her mother with much difficulty by visiting her regularly. When I met her last fall in Seoul, she told me about the difficulty of serving her mother-in-law at home every day and at the same time taking care of her own mother informally by visiting her as often as possible. She said that she felt guilty because she was unable to take care of her own mother at home.

In Korea, not only are boys preferred because they will take care of their aging parents, but boys are also treated more favorably than girls and more emphasis is placed on boys' education than girls'. Many girls in rural areas move to large cities for urban jobs after completing middle school. It is not uncommon for them to work long hours and save money to support their younger brother's high school or college education. Female high school students spend much more time helping with housework at home and get less financial support for extracurricular studies than male students. Because of different educational expectations for boys and girls, there is a big gender gap in education. In 1990, 50 percent of 18- to 21-year-old men in Korea were enrolled in colleges and universities compared to only 24 percent of young women; approximately 20 percent of men 25-years-old and over had completed four years of college education compared to 8 percent of women (Korean Women's Development Institute, 1994: 70, 73). Often, an academically talented daughter is denied an opportunity for a college education whereas her "less-than-average" brother is given the opportunity (A. Kim 1996, Chapter 3).

EMPHASIS ON CHILDREN'S EDUCATION

There are a number of significant differences between Korea and the United States in child socialization (see Min 1997b). As a result of the norm of filial piety in Korea, there is a greater emphasis on children's obedience to and respect for parents and adults than in the United States. Also, under the influence of the Confucian patriarchal ideology, people in South Korea practice more conservative gender socialization, treating boys and girls in a more unequal way than is the norm here. Probably the most significant difference in child socialization between the two countries is that in Korea far more emphasis is placed on children's education than in the United States.

Confucius and Mencius, the two Chinese sages who provided the philosophical foundation for Confucian ideology, envisioned an enlightened government ruled by highly educated intellectuals. Following their teachings, in the third century China devised the civil service examination system to bring men of intelligence and ability into government regardless of social position. Korea adopted civil service examinations in the tenth century. Those who passed the examination were offered high government positions that gave great power and economic rewards. Particularly during the Yi dynasty, which adopted Confucianism as a political philosophy, literary persons well versed in Chinese classics were able to hold high-ranking positions in government through passing the civil service examination. Koreans put great emphasis on formal education as the main avenue for social mobility, because historically the civil service examination provided the main opportunity for upward social mobility.

Under the impact of Confucian cultural tradition, people in South Korea still highly value formal education as a means of social mobility. "You are an uneducated guy (*Nunun motbaoon nonmiya!*)" is the worst curse you can get in Korea. In Korea, a man without a college degree encounters barriers in all features of his social life, including selecting a marital partner. Parents make enormous sacrifices to give their children a good education because they, particularly mothers, largely evaluate their own success according to what college their children get into. Many middle-aged people in Seoul work from early morning to late at night, peddling fruits and vegetables on the street, to support their children's college education.

Last summer when I was in Seoul for research, a well-known artist in his mid-forties came to my office and asked for information about admission to a college in the United States for a bachelor program in arts. I asked him why he wanted to come to the United States to get a college education in his middle years when he had his family members to support. To answer my question, he told me the following story:

> In an exhibition of my art works that was held last year, a businessman set aside one of my pictures to purchase. Before he paid for the picture, he asked me what college I graduated from. When I told him I did not get a college education, he changed his mind, deciding not to buy my picture. It seems to me he did not think my picture was meaningful when he found out I was a non-college artist. This bitter experience, along with many other barriers I had encountered before in my career as an artist, forced me to seek a college education in the late stage of my life.

This episode reveals what social barriers a man with no college degree encounters in Korean society.

Since colleges and universities in South Korea can admit only a small proportion (approximately 35 percent) of high school candidates each year, competition in the college entrance examination is fierce. Korean children compete to be admitted not only to any college, but also to a first-class university, because the reputation of one's college has significant effects on social mobility throughout life. Korean children spend at least three years of high school preparing for the college entrance examination by attending study programs offered by each high school and private institutions after regular school hours. Many upper-middle and upper-class families hire one or more private tutors for their high school children. Despite several years of hard work, many students fail to gain admission to college in their first try. Those who fail attend private institutions specializing in preparation for the college entrance examination. They try to get admission to college again and again under much pressure, even in the fourth year after graduation from high school.

In the summer of 1995, I stayed at my female cousin's home in Seoul for five days. At that time, my cousin had two high school children, one in the twelfth grade and the other in the tenth (the first year in high school in Korea). During my visit, the twelfth grader, Heyoung, had only two months left before she took the college entrance examination. This gave me an opportunity to observe the hardship and torture that Korean high school seniors, along with their parents, go through for admission to college.

Heyoung had a hectic daily schedule, from 5:30 in the morning to 1:00 the next morning, sleeping less than five hours a night. She left for school at 6:00 in the morning with lunch and dinner baskets (there is no school cafeteria in a Korean high school). First, she participated in a two-hour self-study program, supervised by her homeroom teacher, between 6:30 and 8:20. Her school principal mandated all high school seniors to participate in the self-study program to increase the school's college admission rate. Her regular class schedule between 8:30 and 3:00 included a 40-minute lunch break. Heyoung told me that her homeroom teacher stayed in the classroom even during the lunch period to make sure students studied by themselves as soon as they finished their lunches. However, she said that "many students are so tired that they fall asleep upon completing their lunch." Beginning at 3:30, after the regular schedule, Heyoung and other seniors took three consecutive entrance examination preparation classes (English, mathematics, and the Korean language) offered by the high school. Between 6:30 and 7:30, Heyoung completed her dinner basket, then she participated in another two-hour self-study program. She came back home after 10. P.M. She said many of her classmates were participating in a "mid-night extracurricular study" (*simya kwawe kongboo*) offered by private tutors after the evening self-study program. After a light dinner and a quick shower (she said many of her friends kept their hair short so that they did not have to take a shower every day), Heyoung studied until one in the morning to complete her homework assignments.

My cousin got up at five in the morning to make three lunch baskets, two for her daughter and one for her son, and to help the children go to school. After her children and husband left home, she went to bed again around 9:30 A.M. and slept until noon. Her son came home around 5:30 in the evening after participating in two extracurricular study classes (English and mathematics). Fortunately for my cousin, her son was old enough to go to the extracurricular institute by himself. She told me that many of the Korean mothers with elementary and/or middle school kids were busy in the afternoon, taking their kids to English, mathematics, art, piano and/or karate lessons. This suggests that it is almost impossible for mothers with younger children to work outside the home in Korea.

The preparation for the college entrance examination also causes parents heavy financial burdens. Almost all parents with a high school senior pay a regular tuition (a high school education is not free in Korea) and fees for extracurricular studies offered by each school after regular classes and during the summer vacation. Most parents with a school child in other grades also pay for one or another kind of extracurricular course offered by a tutor or a private institute. A large number of high school students from Korea are enrolled in prestigious American private boarding schools located in the Los Angeles area or in New England. As foreign students, they usually do not get any financial support from the school, paying an average of $22,000 per year for tuition, room and board, and other fees. In addition, they pay a travel agency in Korea approximately $5,000 for paper work to get admission and at least another $5,000 for two round-way trips from Korea to the United States (for each student and one parent).

Just two weeks ago, a brother-in-law on my wife's side visited us from Korea to take one of his daughters to a private high school in Maryland. On our way to the school, I asked him why he had decided to put his daughter in a private school in the United States that incurs such a great expense. He told me that many high school students in Korea spend more than $25,000 per year to prepare for the college entrance examination with no guarantee that they will be admitted to a decent university in the first year after graduation from high school. In his view, studying in a private high school in the United States is more economical and easier psychologically because graduation from a high school here almost guarantees a student's admission to a decent university. He and his wife plan to move to the United States as permanent residents within the next three years, before their twelve-year-old second daughter becomes a sophomore. He feels that the United States is a much better country than South Korea for college education and that that is a good reason to venture into international migration.

While the zeal for children's education and the rigid Korean college entrance examination system push high school students to work hard, they are the root causes of many social problems, including excessive pressure on children, heavy financial burdens on parents, and a test-oriented high school education. Recently, the South Korean government has made significant changes in the college admission system. Now, a student's high school records and results of the Scholastic Aptitude Test are considered along with results of the entrance examination given by each college or university. The government plans to make further changes by giving more weight to high school records as a way to liberate children from "exam hell" and to reduce the financial burdens on parents to pay for their children's extracurricular studies. However, as long as colleges and universities in South Korea cannot admit most of the candidates each year, there will be excessive competition for admission to college and all kinds of extracurricular study programs, no matter how much the college admission system is changed.

4

Marital Relations

The vast majority of post-1965 immigrants have come from Third World countries, especially Asia and Latin America. Many of these new immigrant groups show high female labor force participation rates (Foner 1986; Perez 1986; Pessar 1987), although married women in these Third World countries often do not work outside of the home. Korean immigrant women, following this pattern, usually did not work outside the home in Korea, but in the United States many play an active role in the family economy, particularly in the operation of family businesses. The increased economic role of Korean women has brought about significant changes in women's lives in general and marital relations in particular—the subject of this chapter.

WOMEN'S INCREASED ECONOMIC ROLE

According to the 1990 U.S. census, approximately 60 percent of married Korean American women participate in the labor force, in comparison to 58 percent of white married women (U.S. Bureau of the Census 1993b, Table 48). Actually, the percentage is probably much larger. The census underestimates the labor force participation rate of Korean women because many Korean women who work for family businesses or other Korean businesses do not report their work to the census. In my 1988 survey of Korean married women in New York City, 71 percent of the respondents participated in the labor force and 54 percent worked full-time. With the exception of wives of successful business owners and successful professionals (lawyers, medical doctors, and accountants), almost all Korean immigrant wives participate in the labor force to increase their family earnings.

The situation is very different in Korea. There, only about a quarter of women 30 to 59 years old in urban areas participated in the labor force, according to the 1990 Korean census (National Statistical Office, Republic of Korea 1993:1). The women in my New York City survey who had worked in Korea typically did so before they got married. A drastic change occurs when they come to the United States.

Most Korean immigrant women participate in the labor force out of practical needs rather than because of their career aspirations. The vast majority of the women in my New York City survey endorsed the statement that "in a normal family the wife should stay at home as a full-time housewife while the husband should be the main breadwinner." Jung Ja Kim, a forty-five-year-old woman, works as a manicurist at a Korean nail salon six days a week, nine hours each day, while her husband works as a manager for a Korean restaurant six days a week. Her son is a college freshman and her daughter is a high school sophomore. In responding to my question of whether she would like to work outside the home if her husband makes enough money, she commented:

> If my husband makes enough money for the family, why should I take this burden? Without me helping out economically, it is absolutely impossible to survive in New York City. I must work especially to send my children to college. You know about this better than I.

This suggests that many Korean women in this country are almost forced into undertaking the unfamiliar economic role, although they generally hold traditional gender role orientations.

Nearly half of the Korean working women work for their own or family businesses. Consider some figures from my New York City survey. Thirty-eight percent of the women in the labor force worked together with their husbands in the same businesses; another 12 percent ran their own businesses independently of their husbands; and 36 percent were employed in co-ethnic businesses. Working in a green grocery, a nail salon or dry cleaning store—typical Korean businesses in New York—means that Korean working women put in exceptionally long hours. I found that Korean married working women in the survey spent 51 hours per week at their jobs, much longer than American working women (37 hours according to one survey conducted in the 1980s, see Shelton 1992: 39). Those engaged in their own businesses spent 56 hours a week in their businesses, five hours less than their self-employed husbands.

Korean immigrant working women make an important income contribution to the family finances, perhaps almost equal to their husbands, although this is difficult to accurately measure. When two partners run the same business, the wife is usually in charge of the cash register and the husband takes care of the total management of the store. The wife's control of the cash register is one of the central factors that make Korean retail businesses, such as produce, grocery, and liquor retail businesses, successful (Min 1988: 114–115). A grocery store owner in Bayside told me how important his wife's help was to the success of the business.

> I open the store at seven and work with an employee. My wife joins me at nine after sending our two children to school. During the daytime, I often have to go out to buy grocery items on sale from large chain stores. I can go out mainly because she takes care of the cash register. At six, my wife goes back home to prepare dinner and take care of our children while I work with our employee. I don't know how I can operate my grocery store without my wife.

Most Koreans, particularly new immigrants, start with small, family businesses where husbands and wives need to cooperate for economic survival. Large Korean business owners can manage without their wives: they run their businesses with employees and arrange for their wives to stay at home to take care of their children. In fact, Korean wives play a more important role than their husbands in many family-run businesses, particularly small dry cleaning shops and small restaurants. I was a regular client of a dry cleaning shop that was run by a Korean wife and her husband for several years (the shop was closed two years ago). The husband played a marginal role in running the shop; he cleaned sidewalks and received laundry materials, while his wife ironed and altered dresses. The husband, an engineer in Korea, did not enjoy his job at all and was reluctant to talk with customers, probably because he felt the job was demeaning. In contrast, his high school graduate wife seemed to enjoy her job, most of the time smiling and talking with customers. The 1,500 Korean-owned nail salons in the New York area are usually owned and run by women. Some Korean men just drive their wives to and from the nail shop and help them open and close it while they either babysit or play golf during the daytime. They are often called "shutter-men" or "househusbands" in the Korean community. As will be shown later, in the Korean community where the husband's main role is considered to be financial support for the family this kind of role reversal puts pressure on husbands.

Korean immigrant wives can also find jobs in Korean-owned stores more easily than their husbands. Although various managerial jobs available in Korean-owned stores are filled by male immigrants, they are limited in number. There is more of a demand for blue-collar workers. But Korean male immigrants, mostly highly educated, are not attracted to blue-collar jobs in the ethnic economy. Korean business owners usually turn to inexpensive, hard-working, and compliant Latino male workers for these blue-collar jobs. The large number of sales-related white-collar jobs are usually filled by Korean women. Most Korean immigrant wives have received a high school education. As high school graduates, they are not satisfied with working as saleswomen or cashiers in co-ethnic businesses, but they do not consider it demeaning either. Thus, the structure of the Korean ethnic economy has helped Korean wives to play an active economic role. While it usually takes newly arrived Korean

Many nail salons in New York City are run by Korean women. This salon is located in Bayside, Queens, a predominantly white, middle-class neighborhood. Photo taken by the author.

immigrant men a few months to find meaningful jobs, their wives often find jobs quickly and become the main bread-winners.

WOMEN'S DOMESTIC ROLE

How has Korean women's increased economic role affected their domestic roles and their husbands' participation in housework? American working women still bear the main responsibility for housework and child care, although their increased economic role has reduced their share of these tasks (Hardesty and Bokermeier 1989; Kamo 1988; Ross 1987). Korean immigrant working wives bear an even greater share of housework than American working wives. As a result, Korean immigrant wives suffer from overwork and work-related stress.

The results of my New York City survey show that Korean immigrant housewives bear almost all the responsibility for cooking, dishwashing, laundry, and house cleaning.

Only in grocery shopping and garbage disposal did husbands take some responsibility. These findings come as no surprise, considering the fact that few husbands in South Korea take responsibility for a significant proportion of housework. When Korean working women get help around the house, it is most likely from their mothers, mothers-in-law, and daughters, not from their husbands. He Soon Lee is a Korean woman in her late forties who married her Korean husband in New York in 1975. They have their house in Bergen County, New Jersey, but own a dry cleaning store in Manhattan. Her husband works six days a week at the store in Manhattan while she works five days, taking Thursday off for housework. Each day, the shop is open seven to seven. They get up at six in the morning to open the shop and get home at eight. She told me that she could not sleep well without keeping her house clean every evening but that her husband did not help much. Mrs Kim said:

> My husband is a good repairman. He takes care of electric, plumbing, and other maintenance problems. Other than that, he doesn't help me with housework at home. He never cooks or dishwashes. I don't think in his lifetime he can change his Korean habit of not working in the kitchen.

Younger, professional husbands undertake more housework than other Korean immigrants, although their wives still do the lion's share.

Choon Ran Park, a sociology major in a university in Korea, immigrated to this country several months after she got married to a Korean medical student in this country. She worked full-time to support her husband's graduate education at a medical school. She said:

> He does laundry and house cleaning, but he does not do kitchen work, that is, cooking and dishwashing. Further, he does not think he is obligated to take care of either laundry or house cleaning. He takes the attitude that he is simply kind enough to help me with either of the two. Thus, when he com-

pletes his laundry or house cleaning job, he expects me to thank him.

Two other professional husbands, one a college professor and the other an immigration broker, reported that they undertook dishwashing as well as laundry and house cleaning, but not cooking. One of them, Sung Jin Kang, said: "How can you expect me to cook Korean food, which is far more complicated than cooking American food?" Actually, he does not cook American food for his children either; his statement is simply a rationale for not cooking.

In Seoul and other large cities, middle-class wives often depend on housemaids for cooking and other traditional domestic tasks (Choe 1985: 143). In contrast, few Korean immigrant wives depend on maid service, although most spend long hours at paid work. Only 4.3 percent of the Korean families in my New York City survey had a housemaid working part-time or full-time. In sum, Korean immigrant wives spend many more hours doing housework and paid work than do wives in Korea, and most spend more hours in paid and unpaid labor than their husbands do.

My survey results make this very clear. Full-time housewives spent 46.3 hours per week on housework compared to 5.2 hours for their husbands. Among dual-earner couples, the wives' time on housework was reduced to an average of 24.8 hours per week while the husbands' time increased only to 6.7 hours. Working wives spent 75.5 hours weekly on their job and housework, 12 hours more than their husbands did. Since the vast majority of Korean immigrant wives assume the economic role, most work longer hours than their husbands. Although Korean immigrant men certainly work hard and experience a lot of work-related stress, their wives suffer even more stress and role strain due to the many, often conflicting demands of paid work, housework, and child care.

One can observe the patriarchal custom of women preparing food and serving men in group meetings as well as in individual families. When Korean immigrants have a party, several female guests usually help the hostess in the kitchen while their husbands drink in the living room. Work in the kitchen is never easy because Korean families usually cook elaborate dishes for a party. One can observe the gender division of labor easily in most Korean immigrant churches, too. Women are regularly involved in cooking and serving food for parties while men are responsible for organizational and financial affairs.

Korean men's double standard for boys and girls and their reliance on their wives for many services (without offering services to their wives) make an unfavorable impression on American-educated daughters. Korean women often respond to their husbands' unreasonable requests for various services to avoid family conflicts. Their daughters are critical not only of their fathers but also of their mothers who they think "accept a subservient position." Several years ago, Nina Shin, a second-generation Korean student at Stuyvesant High School (the best public high school in New York City), worked on her Westinghouse project under my supervision. One day when we were talking about second-generation Koreans' gender role changes, she said: "I plan not to marry anybody. Every day I have seen my mom providing all the services for my dad and not the other way. If that is a marriage, why should I marry a man." She said that several of her Korean friends at the high school felt the same way.

Of course, Nina's plan to remain single may not materialize. Yet many second-generation Korean women who are critical of their parents' unequal marital relations may well choose non-Korean, particularly white, partners. In fact, college-educated second-generation Korean women have a higher intermarriage rate than their male counterparts. American-born Korean men are ready to maintain more egalitarian marital relations than their parents, but they still cling to traditional gender-role notions.

COMMUNITY RESISTANCE TO WOMEN IN BUSINESS

Resource theory (Blood and Wolfe 1960; Centers et al. 1970) posits that a wife's employment increases her marital power because it provides her with economic and other resources to bring to her marriage. However, how much a wife's employment increases her marital power depends on the particular cultural context (Rodman 1967). Earlier studies indicate that Asian and Latino immigrant women's economic role has not significantly improved their marital power and status mainly because of the traditional patriarchal system they brought from their native countries. In the Korean case, women's involvement in the family business is another factor that must be considered. Unlike paid employment, work in a family business does not give women economic independence from their husbands.

To be sure, Korean immigrant wives' increased economic role has given them more power and status relative to their husbands. Particularly those Korean women who run their own businesses independently of their husbands (12% of working wives in the New York Korean community) enjoy a level of independence and autonomy unimaginable in South Korea because they control personnel and money management. However, Korean women who assist their husbands in the family store do not enjoy the economic and psychological independence that most American working wives do. When a husband and a wife run a business, the husband is the legal owner in almost all cases. This has practical implications. For one thing, the social security tax for the self-employed family is deposited only for the husband, who is the legal owner. Also, the wife cannot sell the business even if she wants to discontinue the partnership because of marital conflicts. Jung Shin Suh, a woman in her fifties said: "When I was considering divorce after severe conflicts with my husband, I realized that I would have had nothing from the business, neither social security tax nor business ownership." After realizing these disadvantages, some of Mrs. Suh's Korean friends recently have registered themselves as co-owners. In the state of New York, even if the husband is the single legal owner of the family business, the wife is entitled to half of the proceeds when it is sold. However, the husband, as legal owner, is in control of how he sells it. One woman I interviewed said that one of her friends did not get a fair share of property settlement after divorce because her husband sold the store to her brother for an unreasonably small amount of money.

In addition, a husband practically controls the money and personnel management of the business, which gives him power in terms of making decisions concerning business operations. Although the wife takes care of the cash register in a retail business, the husband usually deposits money in the bank and orders merchandise. Moreover, it is usually he who hires and fires employees and decides whether the business should be extended. American employed women increase their bargaining power mainly because they bring home separate pay checks. Korean immigrant wives who work for the family business do not have this independent source of income, although they make a significant contribution to the family economy. The exclusion of many Korean women from money management in the family business has important implications for their marital power. A divorced interviewee said that her ex-husband used part of their business earnings for dating another woman, which ultimately led to their divorce. Since she was not involved in the money management of their business, she was not aware of her husband's spending money on another woman until it was too late.

The status of a Korean woman as a "helper" in the family business rather than as a co-owner also diminishes her social status and influence in the Korean immigrant community. Korean entrepreneurs establish associations based on business lines, and major business associations exercise a powerful influence on community politics in the Korean entrepreneurial community. Korean self-employed men, rather than self-employed women, represent their businesses and usually join a specialized business association and engage in organizational activities. Even if the wife plays the dominant role in managing the family business and the husband is the helper, Koreans usually consider the husband the owner. My wife operated a business for several years during my prolonged years of graduate education in Atlanta. Although I only helped my wife in the store irregularly I, rather than my wife, was the one invited to participate in meetings of a business association. Business associations in

the Korean immigrant community consist almost exclusively of male members, although many Korean women are as
active as or even more active than their husbands in business operation. My interviews with major Korean business
associations in New York showed that only twenty-one
Korean business women were affiliated with one or another
of the five major Korean business associations, accounting
for less than 1 percent of total affiliated members.

Successful Korean male entrepreneurs exercise a powerful
influence on community politics through their leadership positions not only in trade associations, but also through other
non-business ethnic associations (Min 1996: 202–207). By virtue of their financial ability, many successful Korean businessmen are invited to be staff and board members of
important non-business ethnic associations. Those Korean
businessmen with key positions in major business and non-
business ethnic associations spend a lot of time and money on
their ethnic organizations. While they spend time and money
on public activities, their wives are responsible for actual
business operations. Although most self-employed Korean
immigrants work long hours of work for moderate levels of
income, many of them achieve a high level of economic success. When small family businesses turn into lucrative enterprises, both Korean husbands and wives enjoy economic
benefits. However, business success often gives social status
and positions only to Korean husbands.

Over the last twenty-five years, several successful Korean
businessmen have served as president of the Korean Association of New York. Korean immigrants in New York choose
the president of the Korean Association every two years
through a direct election. In each election, two or three candidates for the president spend enormous sums of money, usually over $100,000, on election campaigns. Once elected, the
president has to work almost full-time at the office and, instead of getting a salary, he spends a large amount of his own
money for the operation of the organization. This is why only
successful businessmen can volunteer for the position. In fact,
twelve of the thirteen presidents between 1972 and 1997 were
successful businessmen. They have been willing to donate so
much money and time because of the high status associated

with the position. And they can do so mainly because their wives continue to run their businesses to support their organizational activities financially. Many other successful Korean businessmen serve as presidents of various trade associations, and as leaders they expend smaller—but significant— amounts of their time and money.

SEGREGATION AND PATRIARCHAL IDEOLOGY

The segregation of Korean immigrants at economic and religious levels also bolsters the patriarchal ideology they brought with them from Korea, and this is another reason Korean women's economic role does not significantly increase their power and status. Korean immigrants are socially segregated partly because of their group homogeneity. That is, they stick together because they share cultural characteristics and historical experiences. However, they are segregated also because of two other structural factors: the economy in which most work and their religious organization.

As I noted earlier, about 85 percent of the Korean immigrant work force is involved in the ethnic economy either as business owners or employees of co-ethnic businesses. This economic segregation gives Koreans advantages over other immigrant groups in maintaining their cultural traditions and social interactions with co-ethnics (Min 1991). But it also hinders their interactions with American citizens. The vast majority of the employees in Korean-owned stores are either Korean or Latino immigrants (Min 1989, 1996). Since Latino immigrants hired by Korean stores also have a severe language barrier, they often communicate with Korean owners and employees using a limited number of Korean words. It is also noteworthy that Latino workers hired by Korean stores usually hold a conservative gender role ideology similar to that of Korean immigrants. Although Korean-owned businesses usually serve native-born white and African American customers, their communications with customers for the most part are minimal. For these reasons, Korean immigrants concentrated in the Korean ethnic economy have little opportunity to learn U.S. customs, including a more egalitarian gender role orientation, accepted by the majority of Americans. In effect, Korean immigrants' language barriers and unfamiliarity with American customs have forced them into the ethnic economy, which, in turn, further hinders them from learning English and American customs.

Korean immigrants' economic segregation helps perpetuate the customs associated with the patriarchal ideology in the store as well as in the home. Most Korean produce, grocery, and liquor stores stay open long hours—usually fifteen hours—a day, and many stay open twenty-four hours. Most of these stores in New York have cooking facilities in the basement so the husband and wife can continue their work while eating. Wives usually cook in the basement and serve their husbands and often employees. Women are also expected to perform other domestic functions at work. In Korea, female employees usually make coffee to serve all employees in the office. The same custom has been transplanted to the Korean immigrant community. In Korean-owned travel agencies, real estate companies, and Korean community agencies, young women are usually responsible for making coffee, going on errands, and doing other miscellaneous chores not directly related to their work. Younger-generation Korean women in Korean-owned offices who are not familiar with the service-related role of women workers often have conflicts with male workers and managers.

The participation of most Korean immigrants in a Korean Christian church also perpetuates the patriarchal ideology and thus reduces the positive effects of Korean women's economic role on their power and status. Although neither Protestantism nor Catholicism is indigenous to Korea, both religions have incorporated much of Korean culture in their adaptation to Korean society. In their efforts to maintain Korean cultural traditions through their ethnic churches, Korean immigrants have Koreanized Christian religions even further (Min 1992b). The patriarchal ideology based on Confucianism is one of the central elements of Korean culture. As indicated by A. Kim (1996), the participation of most Korean immigrants in Korean churches bolsters the Confucian patriarchal ideology in two different ways. First, the

hierarchical structure of Korean immigrant churches rein-
forces the patriarchal ideology. Like Christian churches in
South Korea, Korean immigrant churches usually do not
allow women to serve as head pastors or to hold important
positions, although women compose the majority of church
members both in South Korea and in the Korean immigrant
community. The 1995–96 Korean Churches Directory of New
York shows that only three out of about 500 Korean churches
in the area have women as their main pastors. Women are
usually involved in fundraising, prayer meetings, visiting
the sick, and so forth, all related to women's traditional roles
as nurturers and caretakers, while men hold important positions that involve decision making in organizational and financial affairs (A. Kim 1996: 76; see also J. Kim 1996).

Second, Korean immigrant churches perpetuate the patriarchal ideology by teaching women their subordinate position in the family and society. Many Korean women—
working women in particular—experience conflicts between
the sexist and hierarchical Korean culture and the more egalitarian American culture. One way they try to resolve their
inner conflicts is by appealing to "Christian" religious be-
liefs to legitimatize Korean culture and women's subordinate status (A. Kim 1996: 118). Aira Kim, a Korean feminist
scholar who also serves as the main pastor in an American
church, interviewed many Korean Christian women to examine how they rationalized male supremacy by accepting
sexist anthropomorphic views of God. One of her interviewees said (A. Kim 1996: 90):

> I believe men are superior to women. If men and
> women are equal, there is always collision. There-
> fore, God made women inferior to men so that He
> prevents collision…. Gee I had such a hard life after
> getting married. My husband and I fought so much
> during our twenty-five year marriage, but I could
> not win. Oh, I was miserable. Now, I've given up. I
> realized that to win against a husband is not possi-
> ble because God made men superior to women.

COPING WITH GENDER ROLE REVERSALS

Far from being a model of stability and consensus, many Korean immigrant families suffer from serious marital and generational conflicts. In fact, I was surprised by the high level of marital conflict that emerged in the in-depth interviews conducted for this book. My interviews with Korean immigrants and discussions with Korean family counselors suggest that divorce and separation occur far more frequently among Korean immigrants than in the population in Korea. Census data support this: Korean immigrant men have a divorce rate three times higher than men in Korea; Korean women's divorce rate is five times higher than women's in Korea (see Min 1997b).

Lillian Rubin's popular book, *Intimate Strangers* (1983), about American marriages in the 1970s, helps explain the marital conflicts and dissolutions in Korean immigrant families. Rubin wrote of how the discrepancy between changes in gender role behavior and persistence of traditional gender role attitudes caused serious marital conflicts. Many husbands Rubin interviewed felt threatened by their wives' increased economic role while many wives had difficulty accepting their husbands' reduced economic role. By now, wives' increased economic role has become the norm in contemporary America—but the problems Rubin described are still relevant for Korean immigrant families. Now that many Korean wives play a more important economic role than their husbands—some are even the main breadwinners for their families while their husbands are unemployed—traditional gender-role attitudes severely clash with reality.

Consider one example of the way in which gender role reversals have led to marital conflict. When Kyung Ja Choi married Mr. Lee in Korea, she did not know him well; her mother arranged the match because Mr. Lee was well educated, with a master's degree in linguistics. Upon immigration to the United States, Choi became the main breadwinner by taking several odd jobs, including taxi driving, while her husband was, for most part, unemployed. Mr. Lee's unemployment was prolonged because as a highly educated man he was unwilling to take the kind of blue-collar job that was available in a Korean business. He tried setting up a few semi-professional businesses, such as real estate and insurance, but these failed. Choi had difficulty understanding her husband's "economic incompetence." When she argued with him, she often screamed, "Why won't you find a blue-collar job in a Korean produce store?" She also pressured him to take more responsibility for housework. This situation eroded the husband's patriarchal authority, which led him to react violently to his wife. When they argued, he often used physical force. When his punch caused a broken nose, she called the police and pushed him out of the house. She is now legally divorced.

I know of several similar cases where the husband's economic incompetence and role reversal led to marital conflicts, violence and ultimately divorce. The men were highly educated and so unwilling to take blue-collar jobs, but they were not business-oriented and so were unsuccessful in running a business themselves. Meanwhile, their wives had stable jobs (many as nurses).

In most other Korean immigrant families, the wife plays an important, if not the dominant, role in the family economy. This increased economic role inevitably enhances their bargaining power in their marriages and this often causes tensions. Han Sik Chang, a forty-year-old Korean man, said: "My wife never talked back to me in Korea, but she began to talk back as soon as she assumed the economic role in this country. After seven years of paid work in this country, she now treats me, not as a household head, but as an equal. How can she change her attitudes so quickly."

Some Korean men do not want their wives to work outside the home, and I found a few women who worked part-time without their husbands' knowledge. But most Korean men in New York expect their wives to participate in the labor force because it is almost impossible for their families to manage otherwise. The men are frustrated over their inability to support their families without the help of their wives. However, they do not accept the logic that because women now work they should reduce their patriarchal authority and increase their share of housework. When I said, "Don't you think you should assume more housework responsibility as your wife, too, works in the shop?" Dong Sik Lee, who runs a dry cleaning store in Manhattan with his wife, responded:

> Of course, in a normal situation my wife should not work outside the home. Now she is forced to work for family survival in a special situation. But how can we, men, change our custom of not working in the kitchen so quickly and maintain equal relations with them [wives]? Further, if marital relations are equal, we will have lots of conflicts. See, American families! They are more equal, women are more aggressive, but that's why they have lots of conflicts and divorces. There is no order in them.

Partly because of frequent marital conflicts in dual-worker families, Korean women as well as men often consider the wife's labor force participation undesirable. As one woman described:

> I deliberately decided not to work outside the home, although it is not easy to stay at home as a full-time housewife. I saw many Korean dual-worker couples having marital conflicts. When women make money they become aggressive and argue with their husbands. In order to maintain order in the family, we need to maintain the gender division of labor and the patriarchal system. This is why I decided not to work.

Korean men feel it is difficult to cope with the loss in occupational status they experience in this country. In the face of downward occupational mobility, they seek to assert their authority in the home, but increasingly they feel that their wives and children no longer accept it without question. Often their frustration over low status becomes serious when they reach middle age, leading to a mid-life crisis. Young Soo Lee, who worked as a manager for a major bank branch in Korea, immigrated to this country in the late 1970s to achieve his "American dream." In his early fifties now, he has been running his deli store for ten years. His wife said:

> He has often expressed his bitterness about his position as a small store owner. And his frustration over his low status greatly influences our relations. Five years ago, he left home after a little argument with me and came back two weeks later. He wanted to get respect from me. But a real source of the problem was not me, but his frustration over low status.

Some Korean women go through a mid-life crisis derived from status anxiety as well, complicating their marital relations. Women may feel that they have spent too much time caring for their families and not enough on their own careers. Husbands may resist their wives' new career goals and independence. I interviewed He Ran Park, a Korean woman in her late forties. She had four children under eighteen but had just begun a college degree program. He Ran taught for eight years in an elementary school in Korea, including two years after marriage, before she immigrated with her family to this country (at that time people were certified to teach in an elementary school in Korea with two years of college education). She spent all her years in this country helping her husband with his business and caring for her four children. She commented:

> I decided to start a college degree program at this stage of life to save myself, to save my career. For so many years I had been preoccupied with child care and family survival. But suddenly I realized that I had lost too much of myself. Of course, my study complicates my family life and marital relations. But I am now so determined that my husband cannot stop me.

She said that the Korean custom that stresses a mother's sacrifice for her children's education victimizes so many women. She emphasized that her career is as important as her children's education.

One way Korean men compensate for the low status associated with their occupations is to seek status in the Korean community by joining various ethnic organizations. There is strong competition and intense struggles for high-status positions (*gumtoo ssaoom*) as ethnic organizations can provide only a limited number of such positions. As previously noted, many successful businessmen spend large amounts of money ("face-saving money") to secure positions in large ethnic organizations, including churches (Min 1992b). Many Korean women resist their husbands' excessive donations and frequent social meetings to get *gumtoo* (a high position) in the Korean community. In one extreme case, a husband spent so much money and time on his election campaigns that he neglected his grocery business and children. To get his friends' strong support for his election campaign, he organized several golf trips and used credit cards to pay for the trips.

Status anxiety and frustration can lead Korean immigrant men to turn to excessive drinking, golfing, and gambling, which, needless to say, contributes to marital difficulties. Soon Hi Kwon, a woman in her mid-forties, commented on her husband's drinking problem:

> When our discount store did well, my husband began to drink in Korean clubs regularly. Each night, he paid over $300 for liquor and around $100 to the girls as tips. Sometimes, he drank until early morning and came back directly to the store. After sleeping in the store, he left for the club early evening with money from the cash register.

Another woman described her husband's "habitual drinking" as the most serious problem in their marital relations:

> Two or three times a month, he is involved in heavy drinking. Two weeks ago, the police called me from a Korean club. Because he did not want to leave the club when they were closing it, they called the police. At 3:00 in the morning, I tried to pick him up from the club, but he resisted. Two police officers

helped me to put him into the car. He closed his business on the day.

My sister-in-law, my mother-in-law, and even my mother in Korea do not consider heavy drinking as a serious problem. They often say, "If he doesn't beat you after drinking it is okay." But it is not acceptable to me. Why do I have to suffer so much because of his drinking problem. If he does not stop his excessive drinking soon, I will consider separation seriously.

Korean immigrants' excessive drinking is partly cultural. In New York as well as in Korea, many Korean men often go *eecha* (going to another place for drinking in the same night) and *samcha* (going to a third place for drinking in the same night) partly because it is an accepted custom. But Korean immigrants' boredom and status anxiety related to their monotonous lives in labor-intensive small businesses also contribute to heavy drinking. They are looking for an outlet for their stress and the monotony of their lives and want to get respect from women in Korean clubs. Hang Ja Kim, the former director of a Korean family counseling center, observed: "With $400 in a Korean club, each of them is treated like a king by young Korean girls. For at least two or three hours, they can release all their tensions and stress. With their blue-collar jobs, nowhere can they get that kind of treatment."

Still another important cause of Korean immigrants' frequent marital conflicts is their long hours of working together. Many Koreans who run family businesses spend twenty-four hours a day with their spouses, often in a very stressful environment. It is easy for them to argue over business matters. Since there is no clear demarcation between family and work life, tensions in one area can spill over and exacerbate tensions in the other area. Also a problem is that husbands can continue to exercise their patriarchal authority in the store. A few Korean women complained that their husbands try to restrict their freedom in the store as well as at home. He Soon Kim, a Korean woman in her late forties, has run a dry cleaning business with her husband for ten years. She commented:

> Staying together all day has increased our chance for arguments and conflicts. My husband, whether at home or in the store, always tries to exercise his patriarchal authority over me. Meeting him in the evening at home would give him enough chance to restrict my freedom. Staying together all day, he does not give me any breathing room. I wish he, like other professionals, could take business trips often. Korean women like professional husbands because they often stay away from home for a business trip.

It is ironic that many women in Korea complain that their husbands spend too little time with them, that they take too many business trips. In New York, it is precisely because husbands and wives spend too much time together that conflicts often arise.

There are two Korean family counseling centers in New York, one in Flushing and the other in Manhattan. They can help only a small fraction of the Korean immigrant families with marital difficulties in the New York metropolitan area. Moreover, Koreans usually do not want to talk about their marital problems with social workers. Korean church pastors play a more important role than social workers in helping couples with marital problems. My survey of Korean immigrant pastors indicate that over 80 percent of them provide counseling for their church members (1992b). Korean social workers are concerned that many of these pastors have not taken psychology and/or counseling courses and that therefore they cannot provide counselling effectively.

5

Child Care and Child Socialization

Helen Min is a tenth-grade student at Bayside High School. She played volleyball for her school team last year. This year, she goes to a Korean cram school in Flushing after school, instead of playing volleyball. Her parents have pressured her to stop playing to make her concentrate on preparing for college admission. Not academically oriented, Helen would be happy to be admitted to a state university in New York. Yet her parents have kept telling her that she should try for an elite private college like Smith or Wellesley and that she should concentrate on her academic performance and after-school programs.

When Helen immigrated to this country three years ago, she felt relieved because she thought she got out of the Korean "exam hell." Yet, three years later, she feels as if she is encountering another "exam hell" in the New York Korean community. To her surprise, Helen has found many Korean cram schools in Flushing that, similar to *hakwon* in Korea, provide after-school programs to help students with college admission. She feels less pressured than her friends in Korea because she knows she will be accepted by a college in this country. Yet she is far more pressured than her American school friends because she lives in a Korean family and in a Korean community. This chapter will look at Korean immigrant parents' emphasis on children's education and other aspects of their child socialization practices.

DAYTIME CHILD CARE

As I indicated, only a small proportion of married women in South Korea participate in the labor force. Parents-in-law usually pressure their newlywed daughter-in-law to bear a child, and thus the interval between marriage and the birth of the first child is relatively short. Once a married woman has a baby, she usually focuses on child care. A mother is mainly responsible for child care, with a father not involved much. Many married women in South Korea live with their mother-in-law, as the vast majority of the Korean elderly live with their adult children. When a married woman works outside the home, she usually depends on her mother-in-law for babysitting. Although fathers become more involved in child socialization when children start school, mothers are the primary care-givers in South Korea to a greater extent than they are in the United States. They usually take care of children's homework and minor discipline problems, arrange their extracurricular activities and meet teachers to check on school performance, since the fathers usually come back from work late in the evening. Many full-time housewives in Korea hire housemaids to do housework so that they can focus on child socialization.

Koreans' child care and child socialization patterns undergo significant changes when they move to the United States. The major reason is the phenomenal increase in Korean immigrant women's participation in the labor force. In the United States, many Korean immigrant women delay pregnancy in order to continue their economic role after marriage, reducing the overall fertility rate of the Korean immigrant population. The 1990 census reports show that Korean immigrant women who have passed child bearing ages (35 through 44 years old) have, on average, fewer than two children (1.78) whereas their counterparts in South Korea have approximately three children (3.10) (Min 1997b). In South Korea, where the perpetuation of the family lineage through childbearing is considered an important obligation of married women, a fertile woman cannot choose to have only one child. Yet, in the Korean community we see many couples who have ended up with the only child—a result of the difficulty of raising children with two partners working full-time.

Although many Korean immigrant women with one or more preschool children are at home full-time, there are many others with young children who spend long hours at paid work. Some of these women depend on their mothers or mother-in-laws for child care. A small number send their babies to Korea to be taken care of by their parents or parents-in-law in the first few years. Many more women ask their parents or parents-in-law to help with baby sitting and housework. Korean couples often invite elderly mothers or mothers-in-law from Korea for a temporary visit before the baby is due, and the older women usually remain longer to help with babysitting and housekeeping. An elderly mother's assistance at home is crucial to the economic survival of many Korean families where a husband and a wife work long hours outside the home.

Hyun Joo Jung's story illustrates the point well. She moved to New York City in 1971 and soon married a Korean man. When she became pregnant, she was running a children's wear shop with her husband in Brooklyn. In no way, would her husband be able to run the business without her. She decided to invite her mother from Korea for child care so that she could go back to her business soon after the birth of her child. Now, at 53, she described how her mother's help at home enabled her to join her husband in running the business:

> I invited my mother for a temporary visit before I delivered my baby. Thanks to my mother I was able to resume my job in our retail store two months after the delivery of the baby. One year later, my mother went back to Korea and I had to take the baby to a private babysitter. He cried every morning when I put him at the babysitter.

> I decided to invite my mother for permanent residence particularly for the purpose of babysitting. The next year, my mother came back to this country for permanent residence and took care of my son, the only child, until he completed elementary school. I don't know how I could have taken care of my boy while keeping my job without my mother. When my boy became old enough, my mother moved to my younger sister's home to take care of her babies.

As illustrated in Chapter 3, the norm of patrilocality (living with a husband's parents) is strictly observed in Korea. However, in New York and other Korean communities it is more common for a Korean immigrant couple to live with a wife's parents than with a husband's. In Korea, a daughter-in-law typically has a tension-filled relationship with her cohabiting mother-in-law, often causing difficulties for her husband, who is caught between loyalties to his wife and mother. The relationship between a son-in-law and a mother-in-law is considered to be less difficult than that between a daughter-in-law and a mother-in-law.

In the Korean immigrant community, married women who live with their own mothers also have problems as they are torn between obligations to their husbands and mothers. Soon Hi Kwon, 44, runs a Korean restaurant while her husband does not work after selling his retail business three months ago. She invited her mother from Korea seven years ago when she was struggling with housework, care of her two children (4 and 3 at that time) and her business. Since her mother came, she has been relieved of much of the housework and care of the children. Yet she has difficulty satisfying both her husband and her mother:

> My mother works hard every day for us, like a housemaid, babysitting and doing housework. Yet I often have the guilty feeling that I serve my mother rather than my mother-in-law and my husband's kin. When I argue with my husband, because of my mother's presence it hurts me more than my husband. Therefore, I try to satisfy him, not to argue

with him as much as possible. My husband often takes advantage of my situation and screams easily at home.

Some Korean couples, who do not have the luxury of having an elderly mother or mother-in-law for babysitting, take their babies to Korean babysitters or Korean child care centers. In the 1970s when the New York Korean community was in its early stage of development, few private Korean babysitters were available and no Korean day care center existed. Thus, many Korean couples depended on American private babysitters and day care centers. Now it is easy to find Korean babysitters as some elderly women in Flushing and other Korean enclaves specialize in babysitting. There are also about ten Korean day care centers and kindergartens in Queens that mainly target Korean children. A Korean day care center was established in 1983 within the Korean YWCA in Flushing. It serves children from the ages of three to five and is open between 8:30 A.M. and 6:00 P.M. It runs bilingual educational programs taught by Korean and American teachers. The director of the center emphasized the advantage of its bilingual programs:

> Many Korean parents like our center because it provides bilingual training before children start kindergarten in a public school. If Korean children are kept only at home before they go to public school, they have a disadvantage in English. If they go to an American nursery, they will lose the Korean language. Our center teaches both Korean and English. Some Korean mothers who do not work outside the home enroll their children in our center to prepare them for English education in an American public school.

A Korean private day care center, established in 1978 in Flushing, accommodates children between the ages of one-and-a-half and six in six different classes, and is open twelve hours a day (seven to seven) five days a week. Chinese and white children as well as Koreans attend this center. The center runs bilingual programs with Korean and American teachers.

The labor force participation of Korean immigrant women increases as their children start formal schooling. In my 1989 survey of Korean junior and senior high school students in New York, 79 percent of the respondents said that their mothers were working outside the home. At least when children become pre-teens or teenagers, parents feel the children can manage after school at home on their own. When I asked the students in the survey who took care of them after school, only about a third (33 percent) said that at least one parent was at home when they returned from school, and another 17 percent said some other relative was there. Most of these relatives were their grandparents.

Many Korean children who have no adult at home go to a Korean after-school center directly from school. The 1996 Korean directory of New York listed approximately 120 Korean after-school centers, but the actual number is likely to be larger. There are three main types of after-school centers. Many private institutes or "cram schools" provide junior and senior high school students with extra education in English and Mathematics to help them gain admission to specialized high schools and good colleges. Other after-school centers, usually run by Korean churches, help kindergarten and elementary school kids with their school work. There are also more than thirty Korean arts schools in New York that provide private lessons in art, music, and dance. All three types of schools have an important additional function: they are a place that children in dual-workers families can go after school. Many of these after-school centers have vans that pick up Korean children directly from school and take them home in the evening. Unfortunately, Korean after-school centers do not have enough security measures in transporting children. In 1994, a Korean child was run over and killed while exiting from an after-school center van.

Still, a large proportion of Korean children in New York are latchkey children who come back to an empty house after school. No parental supervision at home after school is a contributing factor to juvenile delinquency in the Korean community. Parents of Korean latchkey children usually call home in the afternoon to make sure their children study at home, but checking by telephone is never enough to keep the teenagers at home. It is easy for Korean children uninterested in studying to go out, meet friends and get caught up in delinquent activities when no one supervises them at home. Some of these children watch television for many hours each day. Others watch video tapes at home with their friends. Still others, although a small number, go out and join a gang and engage in criminal activities such as fighting, armed robbery, burglary, kidnapping and extortion of businesses (Yu 1987). In 1990, the news that a Korean high school student was found murdered at his Long Island suburban home shocked the entire Korean community in New York. He was killed by one of his Korean high school friends, who was a gang member.

Aside from the issue of parental supervision, the absence of a parent at home in the evening in many Korean immigrant families can have negative effects on the psychological development of children. In South Korea, almost all school-age children eat dinner with their mothers, and a large proportion with their parents, elderly parent(s), and/or one or more non-nuclear family members. While talking with their parents and other adult family members at the dinner table, Korean children feel close to their family and come to learn basic etiquette and other proper norms indirectly. Most white American children in this country, too, get together with their parents at the dinner table. Unfortunately, because of their parents' long hours of work outside the home, many children in the Korean immigrant community do not have a family dinner that involves closeness, sharing, and congenial discussions among family members. Out of their guilty feelings, they often give their children a substantial amount of money each week. Korean counselors have indicated that giving children large sums of money without spending time with them can be a source of children's delinquent activities.

Even married Korean women in New York who are in the work force generally accept traditional gender role orientations that make a clear distinction between men's and women's roles. Most believe that a woman should subordinate her own interests to her husband's and children's. As a result, many women who cannot take care of their children after school because of their extended work hours feel guilty. As one woman lamented: "We decided to immigrate to the United States to give our children better opportunities for education. However, sadly, for our economic survival, I have to leave my children at home by themselves in the afternoon. What is the meaning of my immigration to this country if I neglect my children in this way?"

EMPHASIS ON CHILDREN'S SUCCESS IN SCHOOL

The most distinctive feature of child socialization in the Korean immigrant community, as well as in South Korea, is the emphasis on children's success in education, that is, success in school performance and ultimately admission to a good college for a professional career. Since gaining admission to college is less competitive here than in South Korea, the financial and psychological pressures involved in helping children advance to college are less burdensome. Yet Korean immigrant parents put far more pressure on their children to excel in school and make far more effort to send their children to prestigious universities than do most American parents. Many scholars have written that the emphasis on children's education differentiates Jewish Americans from other ethnic groups (Heilman 1982; Sklare 1971). However, one recent study shows that Korean mothers expect their children to get even higher grades and to spend longer hours studying after school than do Jewish mothers (Rose 1992).

According to Chinese classical writings, Mencius' mother (Mencius was one of Confucius' students) moved three times to give her son a good education. Korean immigrants with school-age children often follow this pattern. Usually they decide where to live largely based on the academic quality of public schools in the neighborhood. Koreans are heavily concentrated in School District 26 (encompassing Bayside, Little Neck and Douglaston), the best among thirty-two school districts in New York City. By 1995, 37 percent of the students in the district were Asian Americans, mostly Korean and Chinese. Many Koreans who initially settled in Flushing and other Korean enclaves in Queens have relocated to middle and upper- middle class neighborhoods in School District 26 as well as in Bergen County (New Jersey), Long Island, and Westchester mainly because of the quality of public schools there.

In New York, Koreans continue the practice of sending their children to private institutions for extracurricular studies after school. There are about forty Korean-run private academies in the New York area that provide extracurricular studies in English and mathematics. They usually prepare children for specialized high schools in New York City and prestigious colleges. In the 1989 Korean youth survey, about 20 percent of the respondents reported that they were taking lessons after school either in a private institution or with a private tutor at the time of the survey. The in-depth interviews, conducted particularly for this book, showed that all but one of the junior and senior high school children involved participated in an extracurricular study program at one time or another. Extracurricular programs are particularly popular during the summer vacation. Private academies in Flushing and other parts of Queens expand their programs in the summer to serve Korean students not only in the Queens area but also from Philadelphia, Atlanta, and a number of other East Coast cities.

Partly due to Korean parents' emphasis on children's education and partly due to their relatively high socioeconomic background, many Koreans born or raised in the United States have made remarkable achievements in school. There are many indicators of their academic success. For example, three specialized high schools in New York City admit students each year based on competitive examinations in English and mathematics. Two of them, Stuyvesant High School and Bronx High School of Science, are the best public high schools in the city. Asian students make up the majority of the students in both schools. Koreans compose about 15 percent of the students in the two schools, representing the second largest Asian group following the Chinese, although Koreans account for less than 1 percent of the city's population. Asian

There are about forty Korean-run private-school academies in the New York area that provide extracurricular studies in English and mathematics. This is an elementary English and mathematics class in Rira Children's School in Bayside, Queens. Photo taken by Rira Children's School.

Americans account for over 25 percent of the students at New York University, Columbia University, and other Ivy league schools on the East Coast—and Koreans are the second largest Asian group in these prestigious universities. Two or three Korean students have annually received presidential merit scholarships given to the two best high school seniors in each state based on school achievements and extracurricular activities.

Many Korean parents encourage their children to apply to an Ivy league school without considering their financial situation. Once their child is admitted to Harvard, Yale, or some other prestigious university, they make all kinds of sacrifices to support their children's education. Often, both partners work extremely long hours and maintain remarkably frugal lives to support their children's college education. For example, Mrs. Lee worked full-time as a nurse during the daytime and sold merchandise in the evening to support her daughter's education at Yale. Some Korean parents with two or three children in private universities have serious financial troubles. In one case, a Korean family had its son attending Harvard and a daughter attending a prestigious private college in Boston. When their business turned bad, they began to borrow money from their friends to support their children's education. They kept borrowing money until they had to sell their business and leave New York for another city.

Why are many Korean parents ready to make such personal sacrifices for their children's education? Partly it is because of Confucian cultural traditions that stress education. Also, Korean immigrant parents are influenced by frustrations with their own low-status jobs and unconscious efforts to improve their status through their children. Many Korean immigrant men who completed a college education engage in a blue-collar business or blue-collar employment because of language barriers and other disadvantages (Min 1984b). They know they cannot improve their own social status in this country. Psychologically, they are transferring their own unfulfilled career goals to their children. One day, I had a chance to talk with Mr. Song, who experienced several failures in his business ventures but who managed to educate his daughter at Yale, in the college as well as in the medical school. Praising his efforts on behalf of his children's education, I told him that compared to him I had not made many sacrifices for my children's education. He said: "You don't need it because you have a good position. But I have neither a good position nor money. I need it because their future is my hope."

While Korean parents' devotion to their children's education clearly contributes to the children's academic success, the overwhelming stress on children's academic achievements has had some negative effects. Academically successful children are well rewarded in the family, church, and the community, but students who perform below average or even just at average levels are not rewarded and sometimes neglected by their parents, church members, and community leaders. A Korean college senior told of how her parents' low expectations of her performance affected her:

> She (my older sister) was always good at school and went to a better high school and a better college (New York University) than I. They (my parents) focused on her academic development and made me spend more time for housework and going on errands. Until my college sophomore year, their different expectations influenced my academic performance negatively.

In my Asian American class at Queens College, a Korean student commented:

> In my junior high school, my parents kept telling me to dream of going to an Ivy league school. Unfortunately, my academic achievements could not match their high expectations. By the time I completed my high school, they gave me up. Naturally, my parents do not take my education at Queens College seriously.

She was one of the good students in my class. Her comments reflect a sense of neglect that even many good Korean students experience because of their parents' high expectations. One person I interviewed told me that a Korean high school student, a daughter of a medical doctor, committed suicide because of "her parents' too high expectations of her academic achievements."

The zeal for their children's education and the blind worship of Ivy League schools also influence Korean churches and the entire Korean community. Korean ethnic churches and the ethnic media recognize the students of exceptional academic achievements with their personal stories. A popular topic among Korean church members during the fellowship hour is discussion of whose sons and daughters go to which Ivy League schools. Korean parents with college-age children are constantly asked by relatives and friends what colleges their children attend. Needless to say, this kind of achievement-oriented atmosphere in the church and community settings creates stress for the average and below-average children and their parents.

Korean immigrant parents push their children not only to attend prestigious universities but also to choose fields that lead to high-status, high-paying professional occupations. Medicine and law are the two most desirable major areas, followed by engineering and business. According to the 1987–88 Korean Students Directory at University of California at Berkeley, 29 percent of the university's Korean students declared their majors in the three science fields—Chemistry, Biological Sciences and Natural Resources—that are generally considered pre-med (E. Kim 1993). Another 20 percent declared their majors in Engineering. One reason for their high level of concentration in science and engineering fields is that Korean students often do less well in subjects that require extensive writing. Also important is their parents' strong desire for their children to earn money and status as professionals. Many Korean parents constantly talk to their children about the advantages of being a physician, lawyer, or engineer. Some Korean children internalize their parents' values concerning professional careers at a very young age. Others decide to major in a pre-med or pre-law subject in order to follow their parents' advice and wishes. But others are forced by their parents to choose a pre-med or pre-law subject, although they are interested in other subjects. Korean parents usually discourage their children from majoring in arts, literature, social work, and education.

These pressures from parents are sometimes more than Korean students can bear. Many Korean students lose interest in studying major subjects that have been selected against their will or without their personal commitment. In 1989, a Korean counselor at New York University reported that about one-fourth of the Korean students there get an academic warning from the school each semester. The major reason for this academic difficulty is that they have picked a subject that is not interesting to them. Korean social workers and counselors indicate that even if Korean students successfully complete graduate school in medicine or law, they cannot enjoy their career if it is chosen against their interest. Many Korean students change their majors, giving up the career choices expected by their parents. Some of these students have ended up having bad relations with their parents for many years, struggling with a sense of guilt (E. Kim 1993). Recently, I met with David Park, a second-generation Korean who teaches history at a prestigious private high school in New England. He told me that his parents wanted him to major in engineering long before he was admitted to the University of California at Berkeley. In an essay "Meditation," written to read to his Korean church members, he described how his decision to major in history upset his parents:

> So I decided to pursue history but I still had to tell my parents. Over the years my dad and I communicated less and less so telling him was almost a perfunctory exercise. For my mom the news that I was majoring in history was the intellectual equivalent of coming out of the closet. She was initially shocked and upset. Then she tried to convince me that I was wrong. And finally she struggled to understand why it had happened. Had she done something wrong, she must have wondered. Upset, she asked me a series of rhetorical questions.

GENDER SOCIALIZATION

In South Korea, gender socialization is more conservative than in the United States. To generalize, Koreans prefer boys over girls and place a greater emphasis on boys' education than girls'. Parents in Korea apply a stricter gender role differentiation between boys and girls in housework and extracurricular activities than American parents. Korean immigrants have changed some of the more conservative gender socialization practices brought from Korea, but have retained others.

One major change appears to be less preference for male children. In Korea, couples whose first two children are daughters usually try to have another child, hopefully a boy. The main reason is to have a son to depend on for financial support and health care in old age. In New York, I know of many Korean immigrant couples who have only two daughters. Korean immigrants do not consider having a son a necessity, partly because they do not expect to live with a married child, whether a son or a daughter, in old age. Moreover, many Korean immigrants believe that in America a daughter will help them more than a son will. As one woman explained: "When living independently of our children in old age, our daughter can provide more services for us than our two sons. Sons in this country, once married, won't have much connection with us."

In New York, Korean immigrants tend to treat boys and girls equally as far as educational expectations are concerned, another major change. Census figures tell the story. In 1990, 39 percent of U.S.-born Korean men and 34 percent of U.S.-born Korean women completed four years of college education (U.S. Bureau of the Census 1993c, Table 3)—the gender differential in the college graduation rate for foreign-born Koreans was 47 percent to 26 percent. It is remarkable that Korean Americans have narrowed the gender gap in education so much within one generation.

One reason American-born Korean women have significantly improved their educational levels relative to men is that they encounter fewer social barriers and see more career opportunities available to women in this country. But Korean parents' attitudes and expectations also play a role. When asked whether they placed more stress on boys' education than girls', an overwhelming majority of the people I interviewed said that they considered girls' education equal to boys', although a few women said that their husbands "unreasonably" put a little more stress on boys' education. The women in particular emphasized that "we should not discriminate against girls in educational opportunity." Korean immigrant mothers' emphasis on equal educational opportunity for boys and girls is partly a reaction to the unequal treatment they experienced back in Korea. He Ran Park was working for a bachelor's degree with four children under eighteen (see Chapter 4). Her comments illustrate this point:

> I was born and raised in a strictly Confucian family. My parents gave favorable treatment to my two elder brothers and discriminated against my elder sister and me. My elder sister was smarter than my brothers. But she was not allowed to go to college while two brothers received a college education.

Instead, my sister (the first child) took care of housework and two brothers. She was forced to sacrifice herself for my brothers.

It is wrong to treat boys and girls differently for their education. I will give equal opportunity for all children. I will give financial support for a graduate education to whoever does very well in college, whether a boy or a girl.

Many Korean parents realize that girls have far more opportunities for occupational success in this country than in Korea, and this is another reason they place as much emphasis on girls' education as on boys'. Korean immigrants with two or more daughters, including those with only two daughters, emphasize the advantages of being in this country for their daughters' social mobility. They are the last people who want to go back to Korea, particularly because of social barriers that their daughters are likely to encounter there. When I visited Seoul last fall, I met Mr. Lee, who had gone back to Korea after about ten years of residence in the United States. As a professional with only two daughters, he has been distressed by the disadvantages and even sexual harassment that female workers encountered in his life insurance company. "This society is not good for my daughters," he said, "I will keep their [my daughters'] American citizenship and send them to America for high school education. I hope they will complete their college education and find professional occupations there."

When it comes to housework tasks, Koreans in New York still treat their sons and daughters differently. A survey of Korean and Jewish mothers showed that Korean mothers agreed with the statements reflecting traditional gender stereotypes to a far greater extent than Jewish mothers (Rose 1992). Also, Korean mothers were found to be more traditional than Jewish mothers in assigning housework chores to boys and girls. For example, 63 percent of Korean mothers felt that setting the table should be done only by girls while all Jewish mothers said that it should be done by both boys and girls. My personal interviews reveal that Korean mothers usually do not ask their boys to do cooking, dishwashing, and other chores traditionally assigned to women while they often ask their daughters to do them. All of my three children are boys. I have heard many of my friends saying, in effect, that: "Unfortunately, you have more work to do at home because you do not have a daughter to help with housework." This statement unconsciously reflects their assumption that girls should help with traditional housework chores far more than boys.

In Korea, parents usually discourage their daughters from engaging in extracurricular activities involving strenuous physical activity such as playing soccer or even softball games. In America, Korean immigrant parents are less likely to differentiate boys and girls in athletic activities. Still, there is evidence that many Korean immigrants believe boys are more suitable for athletic activities than girls. In the 1988 survey of Korean married women in New York City, 22 percent of the respondents agreed with the statement that "it is not desirable for a girl to play softball." The 1989 survey asked Korean junior and senior high school students in New York to list the extracurricular activities they were involved in at the time. Fifty-seven percent of the boys, compared to 29 percent of the girls, listed one or more sports as their extracurricular activities. By contrast, 47 percent of the female respondents in comparison to 25 percent of the male respondents said that they were taking piano and/or other music lessons. Many parents in the Korean immigrant community, as well as in Korea, spend much money, time, and energy to develop their children's musical talents. Almost all Korean immigrant homes have a piano, and most of the children I have met or interviewed had received piano and/or another music lessons at one time or another. But, generally, Korean immigrant parents think it is more important for girls to develop their musical talents than it is for boys.

ETHNIC EDUCATION

Immigrants usually try hard to teach their children their native language, customs, and values, and Koreans are no exception. Because of their monolingual background and cultural homogeneity, Koreans have advantages over other immigrant groups in passing on their language and culture to the second generation. Yet, children of immigrants are rapidly assimilating as they come under the influence of the American media, peers, and school education. Thus, Koreans, like other immigrant groups, struggle to teach their children Korean traditions under difficult circumstances.

Survey studies indicate that more than 90 percent of Korean immigrants use their native language at home and that the vast majority use it most of the time or more often than English to communicate with their children (Min and Chen 1997). Most Korean parents speak the Korean language to communicate with their children, partly because they cannot speak English. However, they also prefer the Korean language as the medium of communication at home to help their children learn their mother tongue. My personal interviews reveal that the majority of Korean immigrant parents, including those fluent in English, stick to the Korean language at home for the purpose of children's education. An American-educated Korean professional described how he tried to teach his boy the Korean language:

> My children can speak Korean fluently because we have used only the Korean language at home. They speak Korean even between themselves. When my boy turned to four, we began to teach him how to write the Korean language. When he started his kindergarten, he was fluent in Korean but had trouble with English. I worried about his English, but he began to pick up English words quickly from his peers and English TV programs. Now at nine he is perfectly bilingual.

It was possible for the professional to teach his children the Korean language almost perfectly partly because his wife stayed at home as a full-time housewife. Several people told me that an elderly parent who lived with them helped teach the children the Korean language. Because most Korean elderly cannot speak English at all, grandchildren almost always have to speak Korean to communicate with their grandparent(s).

It is easy for Korean parents to teach their children some level of spoken Korean because they almost always speak it at home. But dual-worker couples who cannot give their children Korean language instruction at home have difficulty teaching their children written Korean or spoken Korean in the standard form (for example, to show respect and politeness Korean children are supposed to use a slightly different language when communicating with parents and other adults than when communicating with friends). When both parents work, they often depend on a Korean ethnic church for language instruction. Most medium-sized and large Korean churches have established Korean language programs to attract more church members. In fact, about half of the Korean churches in New York have established a Korean-language program (Min 1992b). This means that there are about 250 church-related Korean language schools in New York. About two-thirds of the Korean-language programs offered by Korean churches have a one-hour session before the Sunday service. The other one-third have a three-hour session on Saturday.

In addition, seven major Korean schools established in different areas of New York provide Korean language and cultural education for local Korean children on Saturday. Each of these schools has 100 or more Korean students at different levels. Second-generation Korean students comprise the vast majority of the students in these Korean schools, but American citizens who are married to Korean women or have adopted Korean children also take Korean language classes there. Students' tuition and community donations are the major financial sources of the schools. The Korean government provides a little financial support and textbooks for major Korean language schools in New York as well as in other areas.

Now that Korean students are present in large numbers, the Korean language has been adopted as a foreign language in some high schools and colleges in the New York area. At present, six public high schools in New York City and more than fifteen colleges and universities in the New York area offer Korean as a foreign language. The increase in the number of college students who take Korean as a foreign language is phenomenal. Nationally, 3,343 college students took Korean as a foreign language in the 1995 fall term, which marked a twenty-fold increase from 163 students in 1977 (*The Sae Gae Times* 1996a). The Association of Korean Language Schools in New York and that in Los Angeles have lobbied the College Board to include the Korean language as one of the foreign languages in the Scholastic Aptitude Test II, hoping that this will motivate second-generation Koreans to learn the mother tongue. Sam Sung and the Korea Foundation have given half a million dollars to the College Board to cover expenses for processing the Korean language test. As a result, the Korean language will be included in the SAT II beginning in 1997. Now, not only Korean, but also non-Korean students take Korean language courses. Thus, Korean immigrants have helped popularize the Korean language as a major Asian language in this country. It should be noted that the major reason why the Korean language has been adopted so quickly as a foreign language in American high schools and colleges is that Koreans have only one language. Although there are far more Asian Indian immigrants than Korean immigrants in New York, few schools in the area have adopted Hindi or another Indian language as a foreign language because there are at least fifteen different languages used by Indian immigrants.

In spite of all these efforts, only a small proportion of American-born Korean children can speak Korean fluently. In the 1989 youth survey, only 9 percent of the Korean junior and senior high school students in New York rated their spoken Korean as fluent and another 29 percent as good (see Hong and Min, forthcoming). Although many Korean parents deliberately use Korean at home, their children often respond in English, as is the case with my own children. Parents' effort to make their children speak the Korean language at home and their childrens' unwillingness to do so are a major source of generational conflicts in many Korean immigrant families. In the 1991 survey of Korean mothers and their children, a large proportion of women said that one of their three major complaints about their children was that they were not learning the Korean language.

Korean immigrant parents also try to teach their children Korean customs, particularly those related to children's respect in interactions with their parents and other adults. In Korea, children bend down their heads to give greetings to their parents and other adults. On New Year's day, they give deep bows to their parents, grandparents, and other adult relatives to show respect. They also use two hands when handing an object to adults. Importantly, they are not supposed to talk back to their parents even when the parents are wrong. Most Korean parents try to teach their children this Confucian etiquette, but they have difficulty because they have little time at home and because this etiquette conflicts with American customs. They depend partly on their ethnic church to teach their children Korean customs. For example, my former church arranged for the children in the youth group to serve their parents with breakfast and music annually on Mother's Day in appreciation of the parents' care.

Korean parents also send their children to Korea during the summer vacation to help them learn the Korean language and customs. The 1989 youth survey showed that 80 percent of American-born Korean children had visited Korea at least once and 20 percent had visited twice or more often. International travel between the United States and South Korea is now more popular than it was in 1988. Thus, if a survey were taken now, children who had made two or more visits to Korea would likely account for more than 20 percent of the respondents. The Korean government (the Ministry of Education) and many Korean universities have established summer programs for second-generation Korean children. In particular, Korean immigrants with elderly parents in Korea make efforts to give their children the opportunity to meet with their grandparents in Korea during the summer.

Korean American children learn about the youth culture in South Korea not only through their visits to their mother country but also through music tapes and videotapes. Most second-generation Korean children are familiar with several songs popular among young people in Korea mainly because they listen to music tapes at home. Even those children with difficulty in the Korean language still enjoy Korean songs. Many Korean American children also enjoy watching videotaped Korean movies with their parents or with friends. Korean immigrants encourage their children to listen to Korean music tapes and to watch Korean videotapes, which they believe helps their children learn Korean sentiments as well as the Korean language.

About 70 percent of Korean immigrants attend a Korean church at least once a week and an even larger proportion with school-age children participate in an ethnic congregation. Readers may wonder how Korean immigrants can teach their children cultural traditions through Christian religions. Jews and Indian Hindus can teach their cultural traditions easily through religious education because Judaism or Hinduism is their indigenous religion. But neither Protestantism nor Catholicism is Korean immigrants' indigenous religion. Yet, remember that Koreans have developed Korean Christianity by incorporating Korean cultural traditions into Christian religions and that in their efforts to maintain Korean culture through religious congregations, Korean immigrants have Koreanized Christian religions even further (Min 1992b).

Such Confucian values as the work ethic, respect for adults, family ties, and the importance of education are central Korean values. Through their participation in a Korean congregation, Korean immigrant parents want to teach their children these Confucian values. When I asked a Korean immigrant in his early forties, why he attended a Korean church in the United States although he was not a Christian in Korea, he said: "I go to a Korean church mainly for my children's education. The church is a safe place from crime, drugs, and other juvenile delinquencies. It is the best place particularly to teach my children such Korean values as respect for adults, control of temper, and the importance of education." Korean immigrant Christians usually do not encourage their children to be very religious. Nearly all place more emphasis on going to a good college. One female Christian interviewee told me that her first son, who is very religious, wanted to go to a theological school but that her husband insisted he go to a prestigious university. Many second-generation Koreans question the "sincerity of their parents' Christian faith" when their parents ask them to stay at home to prepare for finals on Sunday instead of going to church (Chai 1997). Yet, they should understand that Confucian values such as respect for well-educated people and family ties are the core of Korean Christians' values.

At least in three school districts in Queens (Districts 24, 25, and 26), Korean mothers of school children have established Korean parents' associations to protect the interests of Korean children. In the last three school board elections, Korean parents' associations were actively involved in election campaigns to get Korean school board members elected. As a result, in the 1996 school board election, two Koreans were elected in District 25 (Flushing, College Point, and Whitestone) and another Korean was elected in District 26 (Bayside, Little Neck, and Douglaston). One of the major goals of the Korean Parents Associations is to lobby public schools to reflect Korean cultural traditions in curricular and extracurricular activities so that Korean students can feel proud of them. The Korean Parents Associations have annually organized Korean festivals in several public schools in Queens since the early 1990s. In Korea, a teachers' appreciation day is held in April to recognize teachers' dedications and sacrifices to their students. The Korean Parents Associations, in close coordination with the Korean Teachers Association of New York, have revived the Korean teachers' day ceremony in New York City for several years. In April, they invite principals of dozens of the city's public schools to a Korean restaurant, serving them Korean food and giving them the awards of appreciation. In the first term of 1997, the Korean Parents Association in District 26 also started a Korean cultural class in one school as part of after-school extracurricular activities. Every Tuesday, lessons on traditional Korean dances and taekwondo are given for two hours after school. Non-Korean students and their parents as well as Korean students and parents participate in this program, which is financially supported by New York City's Department of Youth.

Adjustment among the Elderly

Old immigrants usually have more adjustment problems than the young or middle-aged because it is more difficult to learn the English language and culture shock tends to be more pronounced. However, most elderly people in New York's Korean community are satisfied with their lives here. Despite their claims that they want to spend their golden years in Korea, most elderly Koreans remain in the United States, even though, recently, many of their children are going back. This suggests that the Korean community in New York is better for elderly immigrants than for younger immigrants. How is this possible? This chapter will answer this question. Results of the 1993 survey of 152 Korean elderly people as well as personal interviews with eleven elderly Koreans and three staff members of Korean elderly centers are the major data sources for this chapter.

THE INCREASE IN THE KOREAN ELDERLY POPULATION

Before the 1970s, Korean immigrants consisted mainly of young, economically active people, with elderly immigrants composing an insignificant proportion. Since that time there has been a significant increase in the Korean elderly population. Before the 1970s, there were relatively few naturalized Koreans here who were able to invite their elderly parents to this country for permanent residence. Further, even those elderly Koreans who were eligible for immigration were reluctant to come to this country because there were few Korean ethnic organizations and networks that could help them adjust to American society. However, the percent of elderly Korean immigrants has increased since the early 1980s. The increase is due to the growing number of Koreans who can bring their elderly parents through naturalization. Also, the establishment of the Korean enclave, ethnic networks, and ethnic media has made immigration to this country more appealing.

Many elderly Koreans in New York initially came here as visitors and then decided to file a petition for permanent residency after learning that they could live comfortably within the Korean ethnic community. Young Soon Chung, for example, is a 72-year-old Korean woman whose visit to her children in Flushing in 1989 led to a decision to stay permanently.

> In Flushing, I found so many Korean people, many Korean stores with Korean-language signs. I realized that Koreans in Flushing could live without speaking English and that they could preserve much of Korean life styles—eating Korean food, meeting Korean friends, and watching Korean TV programs. I found that I would not have much difficulty living in New York.

Other cities, without the strong ethnic community found in New York, are less appealing, as Bong Hee Kim and her husband found. They immigrated in 1981 to Toledo, Ohio to live with their son, who practiced medicine there. But in 1987 they moved to Flushing to join their newly immigrated daughter. Bong Hee Kim said: "In Toledo I always felt like a stranger, but here in Flushing I feel at home."

In addition to the increase in the immigration of elderly Koreans, the aging of Korean immigrants admitted to this country in the 1970s and the early 1980s has contributed to the overall growth of the Korean elderly population. The aging of Korean old timers, combined with the gradual decrease in Korean immigration, is likely to magnify the proportion of the elderly in the future in the Korean community. An important implication of this demographic change is that care of the elderly will be an increasingly important issue in the Korean community as it will be for the general population in the United States. Another significant implication is that the two groups—elderly Koreans recently invited by their adult children (hereafter referred to as **the invited elderly**) and those who came earlier and have recently reached retirement ages (hereafter referred to as **the immigrated elderly**)—have different adjustment patterns. As will be shown, the two groups have significant differences in kin relations and overall adjustments.

MARITAL STATUS AND LIVING ARRANGEMENTS

Results of the 1993 survey of Korean elderly people in the Queens area showed that 78 percent of Korean elderly men and 29 percent of elderly women were married. By contrast, U.S. census data revealed that 77 percent of American elderly men and 43 percent of elderly women were married in 1995 (U.S. Bureau of the Census 1993a: 55). The low marriage rate of Korean elderly women, compared to American elderly women in general, may be partly due to the fact that elderly widows have selectively migrated to this country. Whether living alone or with their children, Korean widows have fewer adjustment difficulties than widowers. When living with their children, elderly women can help out by babysitting and doing housework while elderly men cannot help much. When living alone, Korean elderly women can make better adjustments than elderly men.

As noted in Chapter 3, the vast majority of elderly people in Korea live with their adult children, in most cases, with first sons. The migration of Korean elderly people to this country has led to a significant change in their living arrangements. My 1993 survey of Korean elderly people indicated that the majority of elderly Koreans (53%) and a higher proportion of married elderly lived independently of their children. About 12 percent of male respondents and 21 percent of female respondents were found to live alone. Although a much larger proportion of Korean elderly immigrants live with their parents than the American elderly population in general, it is a drastic shift from living arrangements in Korea.

In discussing Korean elderly people's living arrangements, it is important to distinguish **the immigrated elderly** (those who immigrated in their middle years and have recently reached old age) from **the invited elderly** (those who were recently invited by their children). By virtue of their long residence in this country, the immigrated elderly have learned basic conversational English and have gained familiarity with American customs. Thus they have no difficulty living separately from their children, and even prefer this arrangement. They have such language and cultural barriers with their adult children (who came to this country in early years) that they do not feel comfortable living with their children even for a short period of time. I found that none of the four immigrated elderly Koreans whom I interviewed lived with a child. Byung Moo Ahn immigrated to this country in 1970 when he was 38 years old. At the time of immigration, his three sons were nine, five and one year old. Now, at 65, all of his three children are married and very successful in professional careers (two medical doctors and the other a lawyer). Although one of his sons lives in New York, Byung Moo lives with his wife independently of his child. I asked whether he wished to live with one of his three sons. He responded:

> I never want to live with my son. It would be very uncomfortable for me to live with one of my sons. Since we have significant language and cultural barriers as well as generation gaps, we have difficulty spending even one night together. When my son and his wife were visiting us from Florida last time, they spent one night with us. But we did not talk much. It was not simply because of my lan-

guage barrier. We live in such different worlds that I do have much to talk about with them.

The invited elderly generally live with their children for several years and then move out. Often, Korean elderly women initially visit this country to help their daughters with child care and housework, then become permanent residents, and move out in a few years. My mother-in-law came to this country in 1981 at the age of 58 as a temporary visitor to help with child care and housework as my wife and I were struggling with three children, a small business, and my Ph.D. program. The next year, my wife, a naturalized citizen, filed petitions for her parents' permanent residence in this country. In 1984, my father-in-law joined us and lived with us for two years before they moved to an apartment.

Even the invited elderly tend to prefer independent residence after cohabitation with their children for the first few years. Korean elderly people in Queens in particular usually move away from their children when they learn basic survival techniques and are eligible for minimum social security incomes. In the 1993 survey, many Korean elderly people who originally lived with their children were found to live independently. When asked why they decided to live away from their children, the most frequently cited reasons were "because the social security money gave me economic independence," "because it is more convenient to me and my child," "to enjoy more freedom and more quiet life," "not to give burden to my child." In my personal interviews, I asked the invited elderly "if living away from your child is good for you, why do you think elderly people in Korea usually live with their children?" Most elderly people I interviewed attributed the change in residence patterns to welfare support, implying that if Korea also offered welfare support for the elderly they might choose to live apart from their children.

Many Korean immigrants who initially settle in Flushing and other parts of Queens move to suburban neighborhoods in Long Island and New Jersey. However, their elderly parents often remain in Queens with their friends. Boon Soon Lee, a 69-year-old woman, came to Sacramento, California in

1982 to join her daughter, a medical doctor. When her two sons and daughters immigrated to New York City in 1985, she moved to Flushing to live with her second son. In 1989, her son moved to Long Island, but she remained in Flushing. She explained why she did not go with her son:

> My son wanted me to move together. But I decided to remain in Flushing because for my social life my Korean friends here are far more important than my children. I did not want to lose my friendship networks by moving to Long Island. Also, I thought it was almost impossible for me to live away from the Flushing Korean ethnic community where all kinds of Korean foods and services are available. Two years ago, my daughter, too, asked me to live with her in their newly purchased house in Long Island. Again, I declined.

Although most elderly Koreans choose to live independently of their children, my interviews indicated that they would also prefer not to live alone. Instead, they look for opportunities to live close to other Korean senior citizens. In fact, retirement homes seem to afford the best arrangement where there are a large number of Korean residents. For example, Chung Ja Yoon, a 77-year-old woman, came to this country in 1972 and lived with her daughter and later with her son in her first fifteen years in New York. In 1988, she moved to an (American) elderly home in Rego Park. She said: "Twenty-three other Korean elderly people live in the same elderly home and I meet Korean friends there every day." Sung Hyung Lee, a 75-year-old man who moved to New York in 1991 after living with his daughter for one year in South Carolina, said that he and his wife rented a three-bedroom house with two other Korean elderly couples.

Many of my respondents expressed the intention to "move into a Korean elderly home if one is established in Flushing next year and if the rent is reasonable." Eighty percent of the respondents said that they would move into it (65% definitely and 15% probably). Several Korean elderly people I personally interviewed emphasized the need to establish a Korean elderly home in Flushing. Two of them told me that their applications for elderly apartments were approved but that they could not take them because they were located far from Flushing. When I went to the Korean American Senior Citizens Society for interviews, several elderly people asked me to help them get government grants to establish a Korean elderly home in Queens. These findings have an important policy implication. Korean and other immigrant elders would like to live in an ethnic elderly home where they can enjoy ethnic food and social interactions with co-ethnics.

SOCIAL AND CULTURAL LIFE

The elderly Koreans in New York, particularly those in Flushing, are tied to strong social networks. Also, they can cope with culture shock more successfully than the elderly in many other immigrant groups because they have access to numerous Korean restaurants, ethnic stores catering to Korean cultural tastes, elderly centers, and Korean-language ethnic media.

The most important place for Korean elderly immigrants' social life is a Korean church. Whether they live in a Korean enclave in Flushing or in a suburban area in New York, an overwhelming majority (80 percent) of Korean elderly people go to a Korean church regularly. In Korea, 60 percent of them were affiliated with Christian churches, but many who were Buddhists in Korea attend Christian churches in New York. This rate of church affiliation and the rate of church attendance are higher than church participation for the Korean immigrant population in general. Sixty-nine percent of the church affiliated participated in the church once per week and another 25 percent participated two or more times per week. Many Korean elderly people attend morning prayer every day.

It is important to note that Korean elderly immigrants' initial involvement in a Korean Christian congregation is motivated mainly by a desire for comfort, fellowship, and primary social interactions, rather than religious faith. For the Korean elderly who live in predominantly white suburban

neighborhoods in New York as well as in other Korean communities, a Korean church is the only place where they can
enjoy social interactions with co-ethnics and meet their
friends and even their children. Young Il Han, a 75-year-old
former importer who immigrated to this country about
thirty years ago, lives with his wife in his house in Yonkers.
Although he never attended church in Korea, he has participated in a Korean church in Manhattan almost every Sunday for the last thirty years. I asked him what were the most
important reasons he and his wife went to church regularly.
He responded:

> I am not that religious, although I have attended
> church over the last thirty years. I began to attend a
> Korean church to meet Koreans. When I came here
> first, there were not many Koreans in New York and
> the church was the only place I was able to meet
> many Koreans regularly. Although I have lived in a
> predominantly white neighborhood over the last
> twenty years, I don't mingle with white people. I
> and my white neighbors say "Hello" to each other,
> but we don't get together for close social interac-
> tions. My Korean church still serves the same func-
> tion of comfort and belongingness.
>
> I also go to church to see my friends and two chil-
> dren regularly. I play golf with several of my church
> friends once a month or so. It is fun to meet them
> every week in the church. My married son and
> daughter live in New Jersey. We can see them every
> week in the church. Often, after the Sunday service,
> we eat lunch together in a Korean or a Chinese res-
> taurant. Sometimes, on our way from church, we
> visit their homes for dinner or they visit our home.

In Flushing and other areas of Queens, a Korean church
is not the only place where elderly Koreans can meet their
friends and other co-ethnics. Yet the church here still plays
an important role in facilitating elderly Koreans' social interactions with their friends. In the 1993 survey (an overwhelming majority of the respondents lived in Queens), the
respondents were asked the question, "On what day of the

week do you feel happiest, and why?" They cited Sunday most frequently because they could "meet my friends." The survey also included the question, "Where do you usually meet your Korean friends?" Again, a Korean church was the most frequently cited place where friends met.

Choon Ja Yoon (already introduced) has many Korean friends who live in the same senior citizens apartment in Rego Park. But she said:

> I meet several best friends in my Catholic church. We have been involved in church activities together for so many years that we have strong emotional attachments to each other. Every Sunday, I am anxiously waiting to see them. On week days, I go to Flushing once or twice per week and meet my church friends at a Korean coffee shop.

Most Korean churches have their elderly men's and elderly women's clubs, which engage in a number of group activities, including *hyodo kwankwang* (tours organized for the elderly as an expression of filial piety). Many churches provide a two-day *hyodo kwankwang* for elderly members twice a year (spring and fall). Young members usually collect donations to cover expenses for the tour. Korean churches also provide a hierarchy of lay positions, which satisfy the status needs of many elderly members. Occupying most of the highest lay positions (as elders), older Koreans enjoy some of the respect accorded all elderly people in Korea but lacking in American society. Both my father- and mother-in-law have been serving as elders in a Korean Methodist church in Atlanta for many years. As two of a dozen elders in the church with about 200 members, they make decisions on all important affairs, including the annual budget, in their church. My father-in-law, who retired from his high-ranking government position in Korea, would have had a meaningless, boring life in this country without his leadership role in the church. Choon Ja Yoon also served as the president of the elderly women's club for her Catholic church for five years.

Elderly Koreans in Flushing and other areas of Queens have several places other than a Korean church where they interact with their friends. The second most frequently cited place for meeting Korean friends, after a Korean church, was a Korean senior citizens center. Queens has three major Korean senior citizens' centers, and three other New York City boroughs and Bergen County (New Jersey) each have local Korean senior citizens centers. All senior citizens' centers provide a number of services for elderly Koreans, including assistance in filling out applications for welfare programs, health clinics, and translation services. They also facilitate elderly Koreans' fellowship by providing them with a meeting place and many recreational programs. In addition, they provide a number of educational programs, including English and citizenship test classes.

The Korean American Senior Center, located in Astoria, is the largest social service agency for elderly Koreans in New York. One popular program offered by the Center is the lunch program. Operating between 12:00 and 1:30 five days a week, it provides lunch for an average of 200 elderly Koreans per day for only $.75. Some are attracted by the price, while others regard it as an opportunity to socialize with their friends, playing traditional Korean games, such as *changgi* (a Korean form of chess), *paduk* (a game played on a board made up of 361 intersections where white or black disk-shaped counters are placed on the intersection lines), and *hwat'u* (a popular Korean card game), before and after lunch. The Korean American Senior Center also has a Korean dance team that consists of fifteen elderly women. They regularly perform traditional Korean dances for American organizations, including American nursing homes.

The Korean American Senior Citizens Society is the association of the Korean elderly in New York, with about 1,000 dues-paying members. In addition to paper work services, educational, and recreational programs, it runs the sixteen-year-old farm program in the Kissena Colden Park in Flushing. In 1982, the New York City Parks Department allowed the Korean American Senior Citizens Society to use a five-acre field in the Kissena Colden Park for farming. About 300 Korean elderly people are involved in planting vegetables and flowers in the park mainly for purposes of recreation

About 300 elderly Korean people plant vegetables and flowers on a five-acre farm in the Kissena Colden Park for recreation and health care. This picture shows elderly Korean farmers distributing vegetables to visitors to the farm. Photo taken by Korean Senior Citizens Society.

and health care. Remember that many elderly Koreans engaged in farming in Korea. Each year, they give away vegetables to visitors to the farm.

The Korean YMCA and YWCA, both located in Flushing, provide various programs for the Korean elderly. The Korean YMCA has swimming and early morning exercise programs for elderly women. The Korean YWCA runs Evergreen School, an eight-week program for the elderly. It has English, citizenship, singing, and aerobic classes, with each class offered once a week. Only elderly women participate in the latter two classes. As part of Evergreen School's singing class, the Korean YWCA has established the Korean Elderly Women's Choir. Along with the Korean Children's Choir and the Korean Women's Choir, also established by the Korean YWCA, the elderly women's choir regularly performs Korean traditional music and dances for American organizations.

Elderly Korean men in Flushing also meet in two privately run *giwon* (the place to play *paduk* and *changgi*), located in *Union Haninnsangga*. There they can play *paduk* or *changgi* with their friends for two or three hours for less than ten dollars. Elderly Koreans often gather at one of the two Korean bakery/coffee shops in Flushing's Koreatown. Even the McDonald's in Flushing has become a meeting place for some. Byung Kyun Han, a 74-year-old Korean man, works four hours (from nine to one) in the morning at the Korean American Senior Citizens Society. Almost every day, around 3 P.M., he goes to the McDonald's in downtown Flushing, where he meets four or five of his friends. Nursing a $.27 cup of coffee (a senior citizen's price), he chats with his friends for an hour. He and his friends appreciate McDonald's for allowing them to have a leisurely cup of coffee. He said: "They welcome us every day. It is absolutely impossible in a fast food shop in Korea." Many other elderly Koreans regularly meet their friends at one of the parks in Flushing. Many Korean elderly women in Flushing regularly take exercise at private gymnasiums with their friends. Many immigrated elderly Koreans who have economic advantages over the invited elderly take golf tours with their friends.

One of the major attractions of the Flushing Korean community for elderly Koreans is the lack of a language barrier, as well as the comfort of a community that feels like Korea. All kinds of Korean foods are available from Korean grocery stores and restaurants. Several hundred stores with Korean commercial signs are lined up in Flushing's Koreatown. Although Korean commercial signs may be inconvenient to non-Korean customers, they make elderly Koreans feel comfortable and at home. Most elderly Koreans can read Korean-language newspapers and magazines available in large numbers in New York. Four Korean ethnic dailies in New York largely duplicate newspapers made in their Seoul headquarters and edit four or five pages for information and news about the Korean community and the larger society. Most importantly, all elderly Koreans in Queens and Brooklyn have access to two or three Korean television stations that air video-taped Korean dramas and movies twenty-four hours a day, and the Korean Broadcasting Station in Seoul offers a Korean news program through a satellite station at nine every evening. Improvements in media technologies have made the adjustment to U.S. culture much easier by making life in the U.S. more like life in Korea. Many elderly Koreans told me that watching Korean movies at home was their most important recreational activity.

ECONOMIC ADJUSTMENTS

In the 1993 survey, only 15 percent of the elderly respondents reported that they participated in the labor force at the time of survey, 7 percent full-time and 8 percent part-time. More elderly women than men worked, finding jobs as babysitters, housemaids, cashiers in Korean grocery stores, and even as cooks in the Korean Senior Center. Some women offer babysitting services at their own apartments while others get paid to take care of their grandchildren. Boon Soon Lee said that she takes care of her grandchildren, two of her daughter's children and one of her son's, at her Flushing apartment and gets paid by her two children. She emphasized that babysitting at her own apartment, instead of at her grandchildren's house, gave her a greater sense of independence. Some widowed women sublease their apartment bedrooms to Korean college students and cook for them to help pay the rent.

The major employment source for elderly men is several Korean senior citizens' centers where they help other elderly people with paperwork. Upon arriving in New York in 1986 at the age of 63, Byung Kyun Han took the English language course for one year. As a result of his improved English, he found a job working twenty hours a week at the Korean American Senior Citizens Society, for $350 a month. His wife earns $150 per week by keeping two elementary school children after school.

The invited elderly did not pay social security taxes and they have no private pensions in this country. Thus they receive minimum social security benefits (Supplementary Security Income and Food Stamps) and health care services (Medicaid) from the government. In fact, welfare programs are the major source of income for this group. The 1993 survey showed that the average monthly individual income of elderly Koreans was $732 and that welfare programs accounted for more than 70 percent of that income. As of 1997, an elderly married couple in New York receives $840 monthly in SSI payments and an additional $200 in food stamps. A single elderly person gets $560 for SSI and $100 in food stamps. Surprisingly, the invited elderly usually do not receive financial support from their children once they are eligible for welfare programs, although they get gifts and allowances on special occasions such as their birthdays and Lunar New Year Day. That is why the invited elderly usually start their independent residence after the age of 62, when they are eligible for welfare benefits.

Combining their welfare benefits and extra earnings, the average monthly income of the invited elderly as of 1997 is likely to be around $1,000 for single persons and $1,500 for married couples. Living frugal lives and seldom traveling, most of my interviewees were generally satisfied with their standards of living, and none complained about their financial difficulties. In fact, they never failed to mention that the income and health care support by provided by the U.S. government enables them to live independently of their children, pointing out that the government-supported elderly care system is better than the family-supported system practiced in Korea. As Byung Kyun Han describes it:

> The U.S. government provides all kinds of benefits for elderly people. They guarantee the minimum standard of living for elderly people. For the welfare of the elderly, the U.S. is a wonderful country. In Korea, the government provides nothing for the elderly people, and this makes the elderly subordinate to their children.

With the passage of the welfare reform bill by Congress in 1996, unnaturalized Korean residents who have been in the U.S. for less than ten years will lose their welfare benefits beginning August 1997. Anticipating the loss, many elderly Koreans have recently become naturalized citizens. Those with fifteen or more years of residence in this country have

Unnaturalized residents who have been in the U.S. for less than ten years will lose their welfare benefits as of August 1997 when the 1996 welfare reform bill is enforced. Anticipating the loss, many Korean elderly people are taking citizenship classes that prepare them for the naturalization test. This is a citizenship class offered by the Korean American Senior Citizens Society. Photo taken by the Korean Senior Citizens Society.

used a Korean-language citizenship test. Others are taking citizenship classes, offered by several different Korean ethnic organizations, including two Korean elderly centers, which prepare them for the naturalization test. Two staff members of Korean elderly centers told me that the majority of the Korean elderly will lose their welfare benefits when the new welfare reform bill is enforced. According to them, many elderly Korean immigrants worry about the impending loss of welfare benefits, leading to lost sleep and other stress-related problems.

The immigrated elderly are generally much better off than the invited elderly. Having worked in the United States for many years, they generally receive larger social security checks than the invited elderly, and many have pensions and investments. The immigrated elderly are also economically more active than the invited elderly as they have gained higher levels of fluency in English and familiarity with employment situations in this country. In addition, they usually have their own houses, purchased many years ago and thus with small mortgage payments. In general, they tend to live much more comfortably than the invited elderly.

Byung Moo Ahn, a college-educated immigrated elderly with three professional children (two physicians and one lawyer), has his own house in a middle-class neighborhood in Bayside, purchased in 1980. He still earns about $400 per week by driving a taxi cab four nights a week, while his 62-year-old wife has been working as a nurse in this country for almost thirty years. He said that when his wife retires in three years they will have enough monthly income to manage on their social security incomes and her pension.

Do Sun Kim, 70, still serves as the owner of his twenty-year-old import business in Manhattan, although one of his sons actually runs it. He intends to stay involved in the business as long as his health allows him to do so. He told me that the savings of his annual earnings from his business, the sale of his import business, and his social security income will give him and his wife financial security in their retirement years. Unlike most of the invited elderly, Mr. Ahn and Mr. Kim play golf regularly (two or three times a month), and they travel by air with their friends several times a year.

KIN TIES WITH CHILDREN

Chung Ja Yoon, a 77-year-old woman, and her four children (one daughter and three sons) organized a family rotating credit association (*kazok gae*) as a means to get together every month. Every month, one of the four children gets $2,000, pooled from the four. The person who receives the money prepares a big dinner for all family members. This story illustrates the way invited elderly Koreans in New York maintain a regular interaction with their children without living together.

In discussing elderly Koreans' kin ties with their children who live separately, we again need to make a distinction between the immigrated elderly and the invited elderly. The vast majority of the invited elderly in New York have one or more children living in the same city. I asked the elderly interviewees who had one or more children in New York but did not live with them how often they met their children. Many invited elderly Koreans participate in the same Korean church that their children attend so that they see them at least once per week. The other elderly Koreans usually meet each child once per month and communicate with him/her on the phone at least once per week. Since most elderly Koreans have more than one child in New York, they have a few meetings with their children every month. Their children usually visit their parents' homes or take their parents to Korean restaurants for dinner.

The immigrated elderly tend to meet their children less frequently than the invited elderly and are less satisfied with the quality of relations with their children. This is partly due to the fact that Americanized Korean children do not understand the notion of "filial piety," a sense of obligations to parents. Younger-generation Korean children maintain relations with their elderly parents on a more or less equal and voluntary basis rather than out of a sense of fulfilling their filial obligations. Byung Moo Ahn's unhappiness may best illustrate this point. His son in Florida usually visits him twice a year on "American holidays" and he talks with him on the phone about once a month. But he is not happy because he and his wife have to arrange his son's visits and initiate the phone calls. Mr. Ahn feels sorry he failed to teach his children filial piety.

The immigrated elderly's relationship to their children is also more commonly affected by language and cultural gaps. As Mr. Ahn observes:

> A major problem in the relations with my children is that we have communication barriers. My English is not that bad, and I don't have a great difficulty talking with my children in English. But when they do things that will hurt my and my wife's feelings, I cannot persuasively tell them what was wrong with their behavior. This problem is caused by our cultural differences as much as by our

language barrier. I often try to clarify the situation using a Korean way of logic, but they lose patience and do not listen to me.

The immigrated Koreans, who generally have adequate economic resources, don't need financial support from their children, and seem to hate the dependency that was the norm in Korea. Young Ill Han, a 75-year-old man with thirty years of residence in this country, said: "How miserable it would be if I depended on my children economically! I feel sorry for many elderly people in Korea whose economic dependency makes them subservient to their children." Although Byung Moo Ahn's three children have significant earnings as professionals, he does not get financial support from them and he does not want to get it. He said that "although we spent a lot of money for our children's education we should be satisfied with their achievements."

The invited elderly Koreans who live independently from their children do not depend on their children either, even though they have much smaller incomes than the immigrated elderly. The invited elderly Koreans I interviewed reported that their children gave them money and/or gifts (including air tickets) on their birthdays or on important holidays. But none of them said they received financial support from their children regularly. Further, they generally held the view that "since the government provides financial and health care support for the elderly in this country we should not depend on children for financial support." To my surprise, I found that an elderly Korean woman who lived in her daughter's two-family, detached house paid rent to her daughter. She said that "since my daughter pays a large amount of money every month for mortgage payment I should help her with my rent." I also found that a few elderly interviewees were paying regularly for their burial sites, purchased with down payments. They said that they bought the burial sites "to avoid financial burden to my children."

In Korea, even if elderly parents live separately from their children, they still expect to get financial support regularly from them. Their children, too, feel obligated to help their parents with regular monetary support. In the Korean immigrant community, neither elderly parents nor their children seem to consider financial support to elderly parents children's obligations. It is surprising that both groups have changed an important norm related to filial piety within such a short period of time.

LIFE SATISFACTION

Both survey and personal interview data strongly suggest that the vast majority of elderly Koreans in New York are satisfied with their lives in this country and plan to live here permanently. My 1993 elderly survey included a question "How much are you satisfied with your life in this country?" Seventy percent of the 152 respondents chose the very satisfied or somewhat satisfied categories, while only eight chose the last two categories (somewhat dissatisfied or very dissatisfied). Responding to questions about their plan to live here permanently or return to Korea, 78 percent reported that they planned to live in this country permanently and only 9 percent indicated their intention to go back to Korea. My in-depth interviews with Korean elderly immigrants and two staff members of Korean elderly centers support the validity of survey data regarding elderly Korean immigrants' overall satisfaction with their lives in this country and their unwillingness to go back to Korea. In fact, I found that a few elderly interviewees continued to live in this country after their children went to back to Korea for permanent residence.

However, survey studies that included Korean immigrants in general show a lower level of satisfaction with immigrant life and a greater inclination to go back to Korea. For example, in a survey of Korean immigrants in Los Angeles (Min 1989: 64), 57% of the respondents expressed their intention to live in this country permanently and 20% indicated their plan to go back to Korea. Since the late 1980s, a large number of Korean immigrants have returned to Korea every year. Economic improvements and opportunities for professional jobs in South Korea and Korean immigrants' overall dissatisfaction with their occupational adjustments have contributed to the return migration of many Korean immigrants.

The findings that elderly Korean immigrants in New York show a higher level of life satisfaction than younger Korean immigrants and that they are more likely than their children to live here permanently were unexpected. Yet the reasons, which have been suggested in this chapter, are clear.

First, the economic and residential independence of elderly Korean immigrants from their children by virtue of governmental welfare programs is a major factor in their overall satisfaction with their lives. Even if they live with their children, they do not have to ask their children for money. They have realized that they have a new sense of freedom in this country that most of their friends in Korea do not enjoy. Many Korean elderly immigrants are aware that their friends in Korea have conflicts with their children and attribute much of this conflict to cohabitation with their children. Generational differences in such things as food menus, the time to go to bed, and even child socialization are sources of conflicts between elderly parents and their children in Korea. Most elderly people in Korea who live with their children feel restrictions of their activities. For example, they have difficulty inviting their close friends to their homes. Korean elderly immigrants believe that elderly people in Korea have to live with their children because they have no economic resources for independent residence.

I asked Sung Hyung Lee, who has three sons in Seoul and a daughter in South Carolina, whether he planned to go back to Korea to live with one of his sons. His response reflects how much emphasis elderly Koreans place on economic and residential independence.

> My first son has asked me to come to Korea to live together several times. But I have declined his offer to live together. My daughter-in-law is not an easy person to live with. I and my wife will have many conflicts with my son and his wife and ultimately be subordinate to them. Even if we do not have serious conflicts, our children will not be helpful to our elderly lives. Our friends are far more important

than our children for our lives and we have many Korean friends in Flushing.

Second, elderly Koreans show a high level of life satisfaction partly because of their involvement in strong ethnic networks and their access to ethnic services available in the Queens area. Elderly Korean immigrants consider their friends more important for their social lives than their children. Elderly Koreans in Flushing and other Queens areas maintain active interactions with their friends every day. These strong friendship networks are essential to overcoming their sense of alienation in a new country. Korean communities in other cities, with the exception of Los Angeles, and other Asian immigrant communities in New York do not provide as strong ethnic networks and as many social services for elderly immigrants as the Korean community in New York. Thus elderly immigrants in other communities are likely to have more adjustment difficulties than elderly Koreans in New York. For example, according to an Asian Indian faculty member at Queens College, the Indian community in New York is so loosely organized that it provides neither strong social networks nor social services for elderly people. As a result, she told me, it is extremely difficult for elderly Indians to live separately from their children.

Third, the lower expectations of elderly Koreans make them more content than young or middle-aged Korean immigrants. Many college-educated, younger Korean immigrants who always expected to occupy white-collar jobs are employed or self-employed in blue-collar businesses such as grocery, produce, and fish retail shops. They feel dissatisfied because of this "status inconsistency," the discrepancy between their high educational and low occupational levels (Min 1984b). By contrast, elderly Koreans have substantially lower levels of education than younger Korean immigrants. The 1993 survey showed that 47 percent of elderly Koreans in New York completed only elementary school and that only 13 percent completed four years of college. Further, regardless of their educational level, elderly Koreans do not have high expectations for occupational success. They generally have the modest goal of maintaining a minimum standard of living, which they are able to do without depending on their children for support. This situation is considered to be better than what they would have experienced in Korea, so their lives seem better than they expected. As a 79-year-old Korean man said:

> All we need is a place to sleep and three meals a day. Since we live in a room provided by our son, we need only the money for food. And we don't eat much each day. A $740 monthly welfare money is enough for our food. Because I don't have a material desire or a desire for status, I don't have to worry about anything. I always feel happy.

Fourth, the active religious involvement of elderly Koreans also contributes to their satisfaction with immigrant life. The Korean church offers an opportunity for regular interactions with friends and family, but has also deepened the religious faith of many elderly Koreans. I found that most of my elderly interviewees, especially elderly women, were very religious and that their religious faith made them more appreciative of what they had. I interviewed a 71-year-old woman who looked very happy (she smiled all the time). I told her that she seemed to live a happy life. I asked her what made her look so happy. She said: "Believing in God and praying made my life happy. I always thank God for giving me so many things."

Finally, the access to more recreational facilities here as compared to Korea makes elderly Koreans, especially the immigrated elderly, satisfied with their lives in this country. Although recreational facilities are important for the quality of life for elderly people, there are few parks and other recreational facilities in Korea that elderly people can use for their leisure activities. Thus only rich people can enjoy their retirement years with golf and other leisure activities. By contrast, elderly Koreans perceive New York and other American cities to provide unlimited facilities for their recreational activities. As Byung Moo Ahn said:

> In Korea, only rich people can play golf and enjoy other leisure activities. The others just play *go-stop*

(a Korean card game) with their friends and then eat *nammyon* (a cold noodle) in a Korean restaurant. I feel sorry for them. Here in the United States, we can do many exciting things for small amounts of money. We can play golf. We can take trips to other cities and even other countries. My friends in Korea told me I was lucky to have immigrated to the United States. And I agree.

Of course, few of the invited elderly can play golf and take inter-city trips frequently. But they enjoy much better park and athletic (swimming pools and gymnasiums) facilities than their counterparts in Korea.

7

Transnational Kin and Family Ties

In 1972, at the age of 30, I came to this country on a student visa for my graduate education at the University of Georgia in Athens. I came with almost no information about American society and with no relatives or friends who could give me information and advice. I chose the University of Georgia mainly because the American College Directory I found at the United States Information Service in Seoul showed that studying there involved reasonably low tuition and low living costs. At that time, the Korean Airline had only one flight a week that connected Seoul and an American city (Los Angeles). My flight from Seoul through Honolulu, Los Angeles, and Atlanta took about twenty-five hours. Further, it was expensive. I worked for two years in Korea as an English teacher in a high school and a private institution to save enough money (about $900) for a one-way air ticket from Seoul to Atlanta. My first international flight was far from enjoyable because I had no one to pick me up at the airport. I was afraid that I could not get to the University of Georgia safely because of the language barrier and my ignorance of American customs. In fact, I had all kinds of difficulties finding a motel in Atlanta, taking the right bus to Athens from the Greyhound bus station, and finding the foreign students' office at the University of Georgia. Further, in 1972, I could not make a long-distance call to my fiancee in Korea even as often as monthly because it cost me some twelve dollars to talk for three minutes—a great amount of money at that time. A poor student, I often called her collect, which her parents did not appreciate.

In the 1990s, flying to American cities from Seoul is much less expensive, more convenient, and faster than it was twenty-five years ago. Now, a Korean has a much easier time travelling on a student or immigrant visa to an American city than I did twenty-five years ago, because the two countries are much more closely connected in terms of information and communication networks. My brother-in-law visited this country in the summer of 1996 to take his daughter to a private high school in Maryland. He and his daughter flew from Seoul directly to Atlanta via the Korean Airline to visit our parents-in-law and brothers-in-law there first. The non-stop flight took only thirteen hours, and many relatives greeted them at the airport. After spending one week in Atlanta, they flew to New York and stayed with us for another week before I drove them to the daughter's private high school in Maryland. This was my brother-in-law's third visit to New York; I also had visited his home in Seoul twice, in 1994 and 1995. Further, my wife and I talked with him and his wife regularly, once or twice a month. In fact, we had several phone conversations to arrange his last trip to New York.

Clearly, improvements in international travel and telecommunication have helped Korean and other immigrants maintain strong ties to friends and relatives in their home country. Most recently, social scientists have shown a great deal of interest in immigrants' transnational linkages to their home country. Several monographs and many articles (those in *Diaspora* in particular) that focus on one or another aspect of transnationalism have been published (Abelmann and Lie 1995; Basch et al. 1994; Foner 1997; Glick Schiller et al. 1992, 1996; Kearney 1995a, 1995b; Lessinger 1995: 87–95; Rodriguez 1995; Rouse 1995; Sutton 1987). Although several scholars have made references to "transnational families," there is no detailed study of such families, or of "international commuter marriages" in which the spouses maintain separate residences in two countries (created by the husbands' return migration). This chapter examines Korean immigrants' international commuter marriages in New York and a Korean city as well as their ties with kin in Korea.

STAYING IN TOUCH WITH RELATIVES

Nearly forty years ago, Litwak (1960) noted that the increased use of automobiles and telephones helped family members in different American cities maintain strong ties. Today, social scientists are witnessing a similar trend transnationally due to improvements in international air travel and advanced telecommunications. In 1996, 68 percent of Korean immigrants in Queens visited Korea at least once since they immigrated, with an average of two visits. The main objective of most visits was to see parents, brothers/ sisters, children, and other relatives, often returning to celebrate important family events like weddings, funerals, and birthdays.

Korean immigrants who have elderly parents in Korea visit their home country more often. Regular visits to parents, accompanied by one's own children, are considered an important aspect of filial piety. Sang Mi Choi and her husband immigrated in 1982, and her widowed mother followed. While she has no obligation to visit Korea, she went back with her husband for a two-month visit to celebrate his mother's sixtieth birthday. He has also returned three other times for various occasions since they first came to this country. A sixtieth birthday is an important event and many elderly in Korea expect visits from their children in America. In cases when the children are in Korea, plane tickets are sent to their parents in the United States.

When Korean immigrants visit their parents and brothers and sisters, they usually spend several hundred or even a few thousand dollars to buy gifts for them. They buy such things as cameras, athletic equipment (golf sets and tennis rackets), telephone sets, vitamins and medicines, coffees, and liquors (Koreans like Johnny Walker and Napoleon Cognac in particular). In return, relatives in Korea usually buy dresses, shoes, socks, and Korean foods (such as sea weed, sesames, and teas) for them. As the standard of living and consumption levels in South Korea have significantly increased during recent years, Korean immigrants cannot buy gifts attractive to their relatives in Korea without spending a great deal of money. Mr. Choi bought a beech ring for his mother's sixtieth birthday three years ago. Mrs Choi said that her husband was somewhat embarrassed because his brothers and sisters in Korea bought far more expensive gifts for their parents.

In the past, Korean parents objected to international marriages because they felt they would never see their child. For example, my parents-in-law did not support my marriage in the early 1970s mainly because they would not be able to see their daughter. Currently, few parents in Korea would oppose their children's marriages to partners in the United States since travel is so much easier. Now, even Korean foreign students as well as immigrants invite their mothers for post-delivery care when they or their spouses deliver babies. In some cases, Korean immigrants are so busy with their businesses in this country that their parents in Korea visit them and stay with their children for several months. Because of his professional business, Sung Jin Kang has been unable to visit Korea to see his parents and two sisters since he immigrated here in 1984. However, his parents have visited him regularly. He said:

> My parents have visited New York every year since 1985 to see me and my two brothers in Connecticut. They usually stay here for three months each visit. They stay with me for most of their three-month period because of the advantage of New York City for sightseeing. Since I cannot visit my parents in Korea, I spend a lot of time on weekends giving them tours in New York. But they also help me with babysitting.

Improvements in international mail and banking services allow Korean immigrants and their relatives in Korea to send money and exchange gifts easily when a visit is impossible. In the late 1970s when I sent a little money to my father, it

Dong Wan Joo, second from right, has been unable to visit Korea during the past twelve years because of his translation service, which he owns and operates with no other employees. Instead, his parents have come from Seoul to visit him and his family several times. This picture was taken during one such visit in the summer of 1996. Photo by Dong Wan Joo.

took about two weeks before my father was able to get my cashier's check cashed in Korea. In many cases, money would be lost altogether. Now, Korean immigrants can send money to their relatives in Korea or get money from them within two days using wire services. There are a dozen branches of Korean banks in Flushing, Manhattan, and other areas with large Korean populations. Before Christmas and major Korean holidays, these branches are extremely busy handling money being sent to and from Korea.

Retail businesses in both the United States and South Korea cater to clientele with international ties. Korean flower shops in New York and other major Korean centers have business connections with flower shops in Seoul and other major cities in Korea. Thus, Korean immigrants can put in orders at Korean flower shops in New York to get flowers delivered to their spouses and parents in Korea for birthday greetings. Four of my interviewees reported that they had flowers sent to their parents in Korea using this transnational communication sales channel. Also, large Korean grocery stores in New York have business links with major department stores in Korea. Korean immigrants can make catalog-based orders from Korean grocery stores in the United States to get merchandise delivered to their relatives in Korea in a matter of a few days. This so-called "communication sales" has become an increasingly popular technique by which Korean immigrants send gifts to relatives in Korea.

The most significant effect of advances in communication techniques on transnational kin ties is the increased convenience and affordability of long-distance calls. In 1960, Litwak emphasized that modern advances in communication techniques minimized the disruptive effects of geographical mobility on extended family ties (Litwak 1960). It is now cheaper and more convenient to make a call from New York to Seoul than it was to make a call from New York to Los Angeles thirty-seven years ago when Litwak made his argument. Indeed, many Korean immigrants in the United States maintain strong extended family ties with relatives in Korea because they can keep in touch by telephone. Among my respondents to the 1996 survey, about one-third talk to their relatives in Korea at least once a week, while half communicated by phone once or twice a month.

Korean immigrants talk with their parents and siblings in Korea for three to five minutes when they call for regular greetings. But they talk much longer when they call relatives in Korea for greetings on special occasions such as their parents' birthdays, Lunar New Year's Day, and Christmas greetings. Sung Jin Kang, a 38-year-old professional, whose parents and two sisters are in Seoul comments:

> I usually call my parents on their birthdays, *Choo Seok* (the Korean Thanksgiving Day), *Sull Nul* (the Lunar New Year Day), and some *che'sa nul* (ancestor worship days). On these days, I talk longer than usual, about twenty minutes. Often, my sisters and other relatives stay with my parents on these days.

After talking with my father and mother, I also say hello to my sisters and even my uncles. But I rarely call my sisters separately.

Over the phone, Korean immigrants exchange information and advice on business matters, legal problems and their children's education with relatives in Korea. Some even run businesses in partnership with relatives in Korea using fax, e-mail, and long-distance telephone messages. For example, Young Sin Jung runs an information center in partnership with her brother in Seoul to help students in Korea gain admission to American high schools. Initially, Koreans ask their relatives in the New York area for information about their children's applications to American private high schools. The relatives in New York usually refer the cases to Jung's information center. Jung then faxes information about necessary application materials to his brother in Seoul, who contacts the families involved. Once the application materials for candidates are collected in Seoul, Jung's brother sends the completed application packages to his sister in New York, often using express mail. She then takes the application packages to the high schools in person to speed up application procedures. When she receives admission letters from high schools, she mails them back to her brother, who contacts the families in Seoul and usually helps the students get student visas from the American Consulate. Her brother sends information about students' travel schedules to Jung so that she can pick up the students at the Kennedy International Airport and take them to school dormitories or private homes. For this international business partnership, Young Shin Jung sends fax messages to her brother in Seoul at the rate of once a day. When the fax messages are not clear enough, she talks on the phone, often for a long period of time.

INTERNATIONAL COMMUTER MARRIAGES

Many American couples adopt a commuter relationship in which the spouses maintain separate residences in two different cities and reunite regularly. These marriages are referred to as "commuter marriages" (Gerstel and Gross 1984). Affordability of long-distance phone calls and air travel allows American partners who live in different cities to commute to see each other almost every week and talk on the phone almost every day. Korean families can do the same thing, maintaining households in the United States and Korea. The spouses can visit each other regularly— several times a year—and talk on the phone every week. We can refer to these marriages or families as "international commuter marriages" or "transnational families."

Both spouses' equal and strong career commitments have contributed to the establishment of the commuter marriage arrangement in the United States and other industrialized countries. By contrast, Korean male immigrants' difficulties in, or dissatisfaction with, their occupational adjustments in this country and greater opportunities for their children's education here have contributed to the creation of Korean international commuter marriages. In a typical Korean commuter marriage, the husband has returned to Korea for a better occupation while his wife and children live in the United States to take advantage of educational opportunities here.

With this general background information in mind, I consider three Korean international commuter marriages that originated in New York. In 1972, Pan Sik Choi came to New York at the age of 27 to work for an American company. Soo Jung Kim, who was in love with him, followed him three months later on a student visa. After they got married in 1973, Mr. Choi quit his American company job because of his difficulty with English. He soon started a retail business (men's clothing store) in Manhattan while his wife was employed as a textile designer. His retail business turned into a wholesale business in the early 1980s, but it ran into financial difficulty in 1990. At 45, he went to back to Korea to find a meaningful career while his wife and two daughters (one in the eighth and the other in the second grade) remained here. The wife said that it was easy for her to decide to live with her daughters in New York away from her husband in Korea. Why? "Because my daughters, born in this country, would have severe difficulty adjusting to Korean society. Even if they could adjust successfully, this country is much better than Korea for my children's college education." Pan Sik Choi has been working as the president of an environmental consulting firm in Korea that he himself established, while his wife has maintained her job in New York as a textile designer.

When he was 35, Jin Young Suh came to New York with his wife and two daughters (7 and 4) in 1986 on a student visa. In 1989, he earned his master's degree in business management from New York University. He soon established a credit union, serving Korean customers in Flushing, in partnership with five other Koreans, which helped him and his family members get green cards. His business quickly expanded, but he became embroiled in conflicts with his partners over business management. In 1996, he resigned from the company and returned to Korea for a new career. He easily found a managerial position at Dae Woo Company in Seoul. Jin Young Suh and his wife, like Mr. and Mrs. Choi, had no difficulty deciding to live separately in Seoul and New York for the benefit of their two daughters' education here. Their first daughter, 17, was a junior at Hunter College High School and the second daughter, 14, was just admitted to the Bronx High School of Science. Their daughters would have difficulty adjusting to Korean society and Korean schools. Further, no high school in Korea, comparable to those the two girls attended in New York, would match their intellectual levels. The wife, Kyung Ja Suh, bought a dry cleaning business in Flushing to live in New York more or less permanently.

Tai Sik Park came to this country in 1968 at age 29 on a student visa for further study. Completing his Ph.D. program in biology in 1976, he found a teaching position at Cornell University. He had a successful career as a scholar-teacher for fifteen years at Cornell before he moved back to Korea in 1991. Because of his scholarly achievements in the United States, he was recruited to one of the two best engineering schools in Korea, to serve as the chairperson of the newly established biology department. At 52, he decided to take this position, partly because of the attractive salary and fringe benefits (free housing and coverage of his children's college expenses in the first two years). Also, he believed it meaningful to his life to train Korean scientists in his field of specialization. When he moved to Korea, he left behind two sons, one a college freshman and the other a high school sophomore, and his wife, a medical technologist. Having two children who had not completed their schooling was a sufficient reason for Tai Sik Park and his wife to arrange separate households, one in New York and the other in a small college town in Korea.

Korean transnational partners talk on the phone with their spouses on average twice per week. Most commonly, they discuss their children's education. The wives often talk for a long time, half an hour or more, to consult their husbands about educational issues. Sometimes the wives in New York have difficulty discussing their children's education with their husbands in Korea because the husbands are not familiar with the differences between the United States and Korean educational systems. As Soo Jung Choi, with twenty-five years of residence in New York, said, "My husband lived in New York long enough. But he was not much involved in child socialization even here and thus he is not familiar with the educational system here. His ignorance of the educational system in New York often makes me frustrated when I discuss my children's educational issues with him on the phone." The husbands in Korea often have difficulty adjusting to the new occupational culture there. Sometimes, they talk with their wives about their work-related frustrations. Kwang Ja Park said that her husband usually called her when he, as the chairman of the biology department, encountered difficulty in personnel management.

The husbands in Korea visit their wives and children in New York two to five times a year, while their wives visit Korea once or twice. Jin Young Suh, in charge of supervising the overseas branches of Dae Woo Company, often visits his wife and children in New York on business. Over the last year, he has visited New York five times, with each visit lasting about seven to ten days. His wife and children also visited him in Korea last summer. A biologist, Tai Sik Park, has been able to visit his family in New York regularly without spending much money because of participation in academic conferences. Last year he made three visits to New York, two of which were supported by his college. His wife visited him twice, in the summer and during the winter break. Pan Sik Choi cannot visit his family as often as the others because his self-employment in a small company does not allow him to take business trips to New York. He visited his wife and children twice last year, during the summer and winter breaks, on his own expense, while his wife visited him once.

In Korean transnational families, the wives participate in paid work while taking care of their children by themselves. Thus they have made sacrifices both for the benefit of their children's education in this country and for their husbands' careers in Korea. Many of these wives initially intended to go back to Korea to join their husbands when their children completed their formal schooling. However, living apart from their husbands for a long period of time becomes comfortable for them and they come to appreciate the lack of interference in their lives by their husbands. They also become more sensitive to the subordinate position of women in Korea as they witness many patriarchal customs during their visits to their husbands. Thus many wives who intended to move back to Korea with their husbands maintain their transnational marriages more or less permanently.

When I asked Soo Jung Kim whether she planned to go back to Korea permanently when her two daughters completed their education here, she responded:

> Initially, it was difficult to live away from my husband. But, the longer I live without my husband, the easier it becomes to live alone. And now I can see many conveniences of living without my husband. I don't have to cook for him every day and I don't have to argue with him often. My life styles have changed so much in this country for twenty-five years and without my husband for seven years. I don't think I can adjust to Korean society and my husband successfully. I plan not to join my husband.

Kwang Ja Park's two sons are expected to complete their education next year, the first son graduating from a law school and the second son completing four-year college. But she does not want to go back to Korea either, as is clear from the comments below.

> At first, I intended to go to Korea with my husband together. But when I visited the campus, I realized that none of the professors' wives there had her own career and that they did not expect me to maintain my professional career. As a medical technologist and a social worker in the New York Korean community, I have maintained my own professional identity. I cannot live in Korea permanently because I cannot be satisfied with the title of *samonim* (Mrs. professor's wife) alone.

These wives will not have much difficulty living in New York permanently, particularly because their children are most likely to find jobs in the same city or at least in American cities. Their children's permanent residence in the United States is something they and their husbands did not consider seriously when they decided to live apart temporarily rather than permanently.

8

Continuity and Change among Korean Immigrants

Confucian values that emphasize filial piety, family/kin ties, the patriarchal family order, and children's education have a powerful effect on the family system in South Korea—and they continue to exert an influence on Korean immigrant families in the United States. Indeed, it may well be that Korean immigrants are more successful than other Asian immigrant groups in maintaining their premigration culture, including their traditional family system, because of their strong ethnic networks, including ethnic churches, and economic segregation. Yet there have also been dramatic changes in family life among Koreans in New York. As we have seen, some elements of the traditional Korean family system have been modified while others have been retained.

The most significant change brought about by international migration is the phenomenal increase in wives' economic role and the concomitant weakening of husbands' role as provider. A large majority of Korean immigrant women participate in the labor force, most working extremely long hours. However, despite the marked increase in Korean women's economic role, their husbands have not changed their traditional gender role attitudes. Korean immigrant wives are still mainly responsible for housework and child care, resulting in overwork, stress, and role strain.

Further, their contribution to the family economy has not significantly increased their marital power and status. This is true partly because a large proportion of Korean working women work in family businesses as unpaid family workers, and partly because segregation in the ethnic economy helps perpetuate the traditional gender role ideology brought from Korea. Still, it is true that Korean women's increased economic role in many Korean immigrant families has reduced their husbands' patriarchal authority, creating a new sources of marital conflict and sometimes leading to separation and divorce.

There are significant changes in child care practices in the United States as well. In Korea, women who have pre-school children usually do not participate in paid work, but instead focus on child care. When their children go to school, women in Korea stay at home to concentrate on their children's education. In contrast, many Korean women in New York with pre-school children depend on private nurseries or an elderly mother or mother-in-law for child care while they continue to be involved in paid work. Most Korean immigrant women with school-age children work long hours outside the home, leading their children to stay at home alone after school or to go to after-school centers.

There is more continuity in Korean immigrants' child socialization practices. In the New York Korean community as well as in South Korea, helping and pushing children to prepare for college admission is the central aspect of child socialization practices. Korean immigrants in New York continue to send their children to private academies that provide extracurricular studies in English and mathematics. As far as children's education is concerned, Korean parents in New York treat boys and girls more equally than in Korea, although, when it comes to housework tasks and extracurricular activities, they still treat their sons and daughters differently.

The Korean elderly in New York have experienced significant changes in their living arrangements and relations with their children. In Korea, the majority of the elderly live with their sons. In contrast, the majority of Korean elderly immigrants in New York live independently of their children, and it is more common for them to live with daughters than with

References

Abelmann, Nancy and John Lie
  1995   *Blue Dreams: Korean Americans and the Los Angeles Riots.*
          Cambridge: Harvard University Press.

Agbayani-Siewert, Pauline
  1991   "Filipino American Social Role Strain, Self-Esteem, Locus
          of Control, Social Networks, Coping and Mental Health
          Outcome." Doctoral Dissertation: University of California
          at Los Angeles.

Agbayani-Siewert, Pauline and Linda Revilla
  1995   "Filipino Americans." in Pyong Gap Min (ed.), *Asian
          Americans: Contemporary Trends and Issues.* Newbury Park:
          Sage Publications, 134–168.

Anderson, G. and S. Thrasher
  1988   "The West Indian Family." *Social Casework: The Journal of
          Contemporary Social Work,* 171–176.

Basch, Linda, Nina Schiller, and Christina Szanton Blanc (eds.)
  1994   *Nations Unbound: Transnational Projects, Postcolonial Predic-
          aments, and Deterritorialized Nations.* New York: Gordon
          and Breach Science.

Blood, R. O. and D. M. Wolfe
  1960   *Husbands and Wives: The Dynamics of Married Living.* New
          York: Free Press.

Bonacich, Edna and John Modell
  1980   *The Economic Basis of Ethnic Solidarity: Small Business in the
          Japanese American Community.* Berkeley: University of
          California Press.

Caplan, N., J. K. Whitmore, and M. H. Choy
1989   *The Boat People and Achievement in America: A Study of Family Life, Hard Work, and Cultural Values.* Ann Arbor: Michigan University Press.

Centers, R., B. Raven, and A. Rodriguez
1970   "Conjugal Power Structure: A Reexamination." *American Sociological Review* 36: 254–278.

Chai, Karen
1997   "Second-Generation Korean-American Ministry." *New Immigrant Congregations in America,* edited by Stephen Warner. Philadelphia: Temple University Press.

Choe, Jae Suk
1985   *A Study of Modern Families* [in Korean], Second Edition. Seoul: Illjisa.

Choi, Helen
1995   *The Korean-American Experience: A Detailed Analysis of How Well Korean Americans Adjust to Life in the United States.* New York: Vintage Press.

Cho, Hyong
1994   "Economy and Gender Division of Labor." in Cho Hyong and Phil-wha Chang (eds.), *Gender Division of Labor in Korea.* Seoul: Ewha Women's University Press, 169–198.

Chow, Esther Nan-Ling
1995   "Family, Economy, and the State: A Legacy of Struggle for Chinese American Women." in Silvia Pedraza and Ruben Rumbaut (eds.), *Origins and Destinies: Immigration, Race, and Ethnicity.* Belmont, CA: Wadsworth Publishing Company, 110–124.

Eitzen, D. S.
1971   "Two Minorities: The Jews of Poland and the Chinese of the Philippines," pp. 117–138 in *Majority and Minority: The Dynamics of Racial and Ethnic Relations,* edited by N. R. Yetman and C. Hoy Steele. Boston: Allyn and Bacon.

Eu, Hongsook
1992   "Health Status and Social and Demographic Determinants of Living Arrangements among the Korean Elderly." *Korean Journal of Population and Development* 21: 197–224.

Fenton, John
1988   *Transplanting Religious Traditions: Asian Indians in America.* New York: Praeger.

Ferre, Mary Marx
1979   "Employment Without Liberation: Cuban Women in the United States." *Social Science Quarterly* 60: 35–50.

Foner, Nancy
1986   "Sex Roles and Sensibilities: Jamaican Women in New York and London," pp. 133–151 in *International Migration: The Female Experiences,* edited by Rita Simon and Caroline Bretell. Totowa, NJ: Rowmand Allanheld.
1997   "What's New and About Transnationalism? New York Immigrants Today and the Turn of the Century." Paper Presented at the Conference on Transnational Communities and the Political Economy of New York in the 1990s. The New School of Social Research, February 1997.

Fugita, Stephen and David O'Brien
1991   *Japanese American Ethnicity: The Persistence of Community.* Seattle: University of Washington Press.

Gerstel, N. and H. Gross
1984   *Commuter Marriage.* New York: The Guilford Press.

Glenn, Evelyn Nakano
1983   "Split Household, Small Producer, Dual Wage Earner: An Analysis of Chinese-American Family Strategies." *Journal of Marriage and the Family* 45: 35–46.
1986   *Issei, Nisei, and War Brides.* Philadelphia: Temple University Press.

Glenn, Evelyn Nakano and Rachel Salazar Parrenas
1995   "The Other Issei: Japanese Immigrant Women in the Pre-War II Period," pp. 125–140 in *Origins and Destinies: Immigration, Race, and Ethnicity in America,* edited by Silvia Pedraza and Ruben Rumbaut. Belmont, CA: Wadsworth Publishing Company.

Glick Schiller, Nina, Linda Basch, and Cristina Blanc-Szanton (eds.)
1992   *Toward a Transnational Perspective on Migration: Race, Class, Ethnicity, and Nationalism Reconsidered.* New York: New York Academy of Science.
1996   "From Immigrant to Transmigrant: Theorizing Transnational Migration." *Anthropological Quarterly* 68: 48–63.

Gold, Steve
1992   *Refugee Communities: A Comparative Field Study.* Newbury Park: Sage Publications.
1995   *From the Workers' State to the Golden State: Jews from the Former Soviet Union in California.* Boston: Allyn and Bacon.

Hardesty, Constance and Janet Bokermeier
  1989   "Finding Time and Making Do: Distribution of House-
          hold Labor in Nonmetropolitan Marriages." *Journal of
          Marriage and the Family* 51: 253–267.

Heilman, Samuel
  1982   "The Sociology of American Jewry: The Last 10 Years."
          Annual Review of Sociology 8: 135–160.

Hondagneu-Sotelo, Pierrette
  1994   *Gendered Transitions: Mexican Experiences of Immigration.*
          Berkeley: University of California Press.

Hong, Joann and Pyong Gap Min
  In press.   "Ethnic Attachment among Korean High School Stu-
          dents In New York." *Amerasia Journal* 24.

Hurh, Won Moo and Kwang Chung Kim
  1988   "Uprooting and Adjustment: A Sociological Study of
          Korean Immigrants' Mental Health." Final Report Sub-
          mitted to National Institute of Mental Health, U.S.
          Department of Health and Human Services.
  1990   "Religious Participation of Korean Immigrants in the
          United States." *Journal of the Scientific Study of Religion* 19:
          19–34.

Janeli, Roger L. and Dawnhee Yim Janeli
  1982   *Ancestor Worship and Korean Society.* Stanford, CA: Stan-
          ford University Press.

Kamo, Yoshinori
  1988   "Determinants of Household Division of Labor." *Journal
          of Family Issues* 9: 177–200.

Kearney, Michael
  1995a   "The Effects of Transnational Culture, Economy, and
          Migration on Mixtec Identity in Oaxacalifornia," pp. 226–
          243 in *The Bubbling Cauldron: Race, Ethnicity, and The Urban
          Crisis,* edited by Michael Peter Smith and Joe Freagin.
          Minneapolis: University of Minnesota Press.
  1995b   "The Local and the Global: The Anthropology of Global-
          ization and Transnationalism." *Annual Review of Anthro-
          pology* 24: 547–565.

Kibria, Nazli
  1993   *Family Tightrope: The Changing Lives of Vietnamese Ameri-
          cans.* Princeton, NJ: Princeton University Press.

Kim, Ai Ra
1996 *Women Struggling for A New Life: The Role of Religion in the Cultural Passage from Korea to America.* Albany, NY: State University of New York Press.

Kim, Bok-Lim
1978 *The Asian Americans: Changing Patterns, Changing Needs.* Monteclair, NJ: The Association of Korean Christian Scholars in North America.

Kim, Byong-suh
1994 "Value Orientations and Sex-Gender Role Attitudes: On the Comparability of Koreans and Americans." in Hyong Cho and Oil-wha Chang (eds.), *Gender Division of Labor in Korea.* Seoul: Ewha Women's University Press, 227–255.

Kim, Eun-Young
1993 "Career Choice among Second-Generation Korean Americans: Reflections of A Cultural Model of Success." *Anthropology and Education Quarterly* 24: 224–248.

Kim, Hyun Sook and Pyong Gap Min
1992 "The Post-Korean Immigrants: Their Characteristics and Settlement Patterns." *Korea Journal of Population and Development* 21: 121–144.

Kim, Illsoo
1981 *New Urban Immigrants: The Korean Community in New York.* Princeton, N.J.: Princeton University Press.

Kim, Jung Ha
1996 "The Labor of Compassion: Voices of 'Churched' Korean American Women." *Amerasia Journal* 22 (1): 93–105.

Kim, Kwang Chung and Won Moo Hurh
1988 "The Burden of Double Roles: Korean Wives in the U.S.A." *Ethnic and Racial Studies* 11: 151–167.

Kim, Kwang Chung, Won Moo Hurh, and Shin Kim
1993 "Generational Differences in Korean Immigrants' Life Conditions in the United States." *Sociological Perspectives* 36: 257–270.

Korean Association of New York
1985 *The History of the Korean Association of New York.* New York: The Korean Association of New York.

Korean Women's Development Institute
1994   *Statistical Yearbook on Women.* Seoul: Korean Women's
        Development Institute.

LaRossa, Ralph and J. H. Wolf
1985   "On Quantitative Family Research." *Journal of Marriage
        and the Family* 47: 531–541.

Lessinger, Johanna
1995   *From the Ganges to the Hudson: Asian Indians in New York
        City.* Boston: Allyn and Bacon.

Lie, John
1995   "From International Migration to Transnational Diaspo-
        ra." *Contemporary Sociology* 24: 303–306.

Light, Ivan and Elizabeth Roach
1996   "Self-Employment: Mobility Ladder or Economic Life-
        boat?" pp. 193–214 in *Ethnic Los Angeles,* edited by Roger
        Waldinger and Mehdi Bozorgmehr. New York: Russell
        Sage Foundation.

Light, Ivan and Carolyn Rosenstein
1995   *Race, Ethnicity, and Entrepreneurship in Urban America.*
        New York: Aldine De Gruyter.

Light, Ivan, Georges Sabagh, Mehdi Bozorgmehr, and Claudia
        Der-Martirosian
1994   "Beyond the Ethnic Enclave." *Social Problems* 41: 65–80.

Litwak, Eugene
1960   "Geographical Mobility and Extended Family Cohesion."
        American Sociological Review 24: 385–394.

Liu, William, Maryanne Lamann, and Alicia Murata
1979   *Transition to Nowhere: Vietnamese Refugees in America.*
        Nashville: Charter House.

McAdoo, Hariette (ed.)
1993   *Family Ethnicity: Strength in Diversity.* Newbury Park:
        Sage Publications.

Min, Pyong Gap
1984a   "An Exploratory Study of Kin Ties among Korean Immi-
        grant Families in Atlanta." *Journal of Comparative Family
        Studies* 15: 59–75.
1984b   "From White-Collar Occupations to Small Business:
        Korean immigrants' Occupational Adjustment." *Sociologi-
        cal Quarterly* 25: 333–352.
1986–87 "Filipino and Korean Immigrants in Small Business: A
        Comparative Analysis." *Amerasia Journal* 13 (1): 53–72.

1987   "Factors Contributing to Ethnic Business: A Comprehensive Synthesis." *International Journal of Comparative Sociology* 28: 173–193.

1988   *Ethnic Business Enterprise: Korean Small Business in Atlanta.* Staten Island: Center for Migration Studies.

1989   "Some Positive Functions of Ethnic Business for an Immigrant Community: Koreans in Los Angeles." Final Report Submitted to National Science Foundation.

1991   "Cultural and Economic Boundaries of Korean Ethnicity: A Comparative Analysis." *Ethnic and Racial Studies* 14: 225–241.

1992a   "Korean Immigrant Wives' Overwork." *Korea Journal of Population and Development* 24: 23–36.

1992b   "The Structure and Social Functions of Korean Immigrants Churches in the United States." *International Migration Review* 26: 1370–1394.

1993   "Korean Immigrants in Los Angeles," pp. 185–204 in *Immigration and Entrepreneurship: Culture, Capital, and Ethnic Networks,* edited by Ivan Light and Parminder Bhachu. New York: Transaction Publishers.

1995a   "Korean Americans," pp. 199–231 in *Asian Americans: Contemporary Trends and Issues,* edited by Pyong Gap Min. Newbury Park: Sage Publications.

1995b   "Relations between Korean Immigrant Parents and Children." *The Academy Review of Korean Studies* 18: 119–136.

1996   *Caught in the Middle: Korean Communities in New York and Los Angeles.* Berkeley: University of California Press.

1997a   "Korean Immigrant Wives' Economic Role, Marital Power, and Status," in *Women and Work: Race, Ethnicity, and Class,* edited by Elizabeth Higginbotham and Mary Romero. Newbury Park: Sage Publications.

1997b   "The Korean American Family," pp. 199–229 in *Ethnic Families in America: Patterns and Variations,* edited by Charles Mindel, Robert Habenstein, and James Wright, Jr. New York: Elsevier.

Min, Pyong Gap and Lucie Chen
1997   "A Comparison of Chinese, Indian, and Korean Immigrants' Ethnic Attachment." Paper Presented at the Annual Meeting of the American Sociological Association, Toronto.

Mindel, Charles, Robert Habenstein, and Roosevelt Wright Jr.
1988   *Ethnic Families in America: Patterns and Variations.* New York: Elsevier.

National Statistical Office, Republic of Korea
  1993   *1990 Population and Housing Census Report,* vol. 6: *Economic Activity.* Seoul: National Statistical Office, Republic of Korea.

Nivison, D. and A. Wright (Eds.)
  1959   *Confucianism in Action.* Stanford, CA: Stanford University Press.

Pak, Chong-Hong
  1983   "Historical Review of Korean Confucianism," pp. 60–81 in *Main Currents of Korean Thought,* edited by the Korean National Commission for UNESCO. Seoul, Korea: The Sisayongosa Publishers.

Park, Insook Han, James Fawcett, Fred Arnold, and Robert Gardner
  1990   "Korean Immigrants and U.S. Immigration Policy: A Predeparture Perspective." Papers of the East-West Population Institute, No.114. Honolulu: East-West Center.

Park, Insook Han and Lee-Jay Cho
  1994   "Confucianism and the Korean Family." *Journal of Comparative Family Studies* 26: 117–134.

Patterson, Wayne
  1987   *The Korean Frontier in Hawaii: Immigration to Hawaii, 1896–1910.* Honolulu: University of California Press.

Perez, Lisandro
  1986   "Immigrants' Economic Adjustment and Family Organization: The Cuban Success Reexamined." *International Migration Review* 20: 4–20.

Pessar, Patricia R.
  1987   "The Dominicans: Women in the Household and the Garment Industry," pp. 103–129 in *New Immigrants in New York,* edited by Nancy Foner. New York: Columbia University Press.

Pido, Antonio
  1986   *The Filipinos in America.* Staten Island: Center for Migration Studies.

Portes, Alejandro and Ruben Rumbaut
  1990   *Immigrant America: A Portrait.* Berkeley: University of California Press.

Reitz, Jeffery
  1980   *The Survival of Ethnic Groups.* Toronto: McGraw Hill.

Rodman, Hyman
1967 "Marital Power in France, Greece, Yugoslavia, and the United States: A Cross-National Discussion." *Journal of Marriage and the Family* 29: 320–324.

Rodriguez, Nestor P.
1995 "The Real 'New World Order': The Globalization of Racial and Ethnic Relations in the Late Twentieth Century," pp. 211–225 in *The Bubbling Cauldron: Race, Ethnicity, and the Urban Crisis,* edited by Michael Peter Smith and Joe Feagin. Minneapolis: University of Minnesota Press.

Rose, Jeshua
1992 "A Comparison of Korean Immigrants and Jewish Families in Child Socialization." Paper Selected as a Semi-Finalist at the Westinghouse Science Competition for High School Seniors.

Rosenthal, Elizabeth
1995 "Competition and Cutbacks Hurt Foreign Doctors in U.S." *The New York Times,* November 7.

Ross, Catherine
1987 "The Division of Labor at Home." *Social Forces* 65: 816–833.

Rouse, Roger
1995 "Thinking Through Transnationalism: Notes on the Cultural Politics of Class Relations in the Contemporary United States." *Public Culture* 7: 353–402.

Rubin, Lillian
1976 *Worlds of Pain: Life in the Working-Class Family.* New York: Basic Books, Inc.
1983 *Intimate Strangers: Men and Women Together.* New York: Harper and Row Publishers.

Rumbaut, Ruben
1994 "Origins and Destinies: Immigration to the United States since World War II." *Sociological Forum* 9: 583–621.

The Sae Gae Times
1996a "The Korean Language Has Become Popular in American Colleges." *The Sae Gae Times,* October 17.
1996b "Koreans Compose 30% of the Students in the Fort Lee School District." *The Sae Gae Times,* November 13.

Sewell-Cocker, B., J. Hamilton Collins, and E. Fein
1985 "Social Work Practice with West Indian Immigrants." *Social Casework* 66: 563–567.

Shelton, Beth Ann
  1992   *Women, Men and Time.* New York: Greenwood Press.

Sklare, Marshall
  1971   *America's Jews.* Brattlebor, Vermont: The Book Press.

Sluzki, L. E.
  1979   "Migration and Family Conflicts." *Family Process* 18: 381–394.

Song-Kim, Young
  1992   "Battered Korean Women in Urban United States," pp. 213–226 in *Social Work Practice with Asian Americans,* edited by Sharlene M. Furuto et al. Newbury Park, CA: Sage Publications.

Sung, Betty Lee
  1987   *The Adjustment Experience of Chinese Immigrant Children in New York City.* New York: Center for Migration Studies.

Sutton, Constance
  1987   "The Carribeanization of New York City and the Emergence of a Transnational Socio-cultural System," pp. 25–29 in *Caribbean Life in New York City,* edited by Constance Sutton and Elsa Chaney. New York: Center for Migration Studies.

Tomasi, S. M. and M. H. Engel
  1970   *The Italian Experience in the United States.* Staten Island: Center for Migration Studies.

Turner, Jonathan and Edna Bonacich
  1980   "Toward a Composite Theory of Middleman Minorities." *Ethnicity* 7 (2): 144–158.

U.S. Bureau of the Census
  1993a   *The 1990 Census of Population, General Population Characteristics, United States* (CP-1-1). Washington, D.C.: U.S. Government Printing Office.
  1993b   *The 1990 Census of Population, General Population Characteristics, United States* (CP-2-1). Washington, DC: U.S. Government Printing Office.
  1993c   *The 1990 Census of Populations, Asians and Pacific Islanders in the United States* (CP-3-5). Washington, DC: U.S. Government Printing Office.
  1995   *Statistical Abstracts of the United States: 1995,* 115th Edition. Washington, D.C.: U.S. Government Printing Office.

Waldinger, Roger, Howard Aldrich, Robin Ward, and Associates
  1990   *Ethnic Entrepreneurs: Immigrant Business in Industrial Societies.* Newbury Park: Sage Publications.

Warner, Stephen
  1994   "The Place of the Congregation in the Contemporary American Religious Configuration," pp. 245–272 in *The Congregation in American Life,* edited by James Lewis and James Wind. Chicago: University of Chicago Press.

Warner, W. L. and L. Srole
  1945   *The Social System of American Ethnic Groups.* New Haven: Yale University Press.

Wong, Morrison
  1988   "The Chinese American Family," pp. 230–256 in *Ethnic Families in America: Patterns and Variations,* Third Edition, edited by Charles Mindel, Robert Habenstein, and Roosevelt Wright, Jr. New York: Elsevier.

Yoon, In-Jin
  1993   *The Social Origins of Korean Immigration to the United States from 1965 to the Present.* Paper No. 121. Honolulu: East-West Center.

Yu, Eui-Young
  1985   "Koreatown, Los Angeles: Emergence of a New Inner-City Ethnic Community." *Bulletin of Population and Development Studies Center* 14: 29–44.
  1987   *Junevile Delinquency in the Korean Community of Los Angeles.* Los Angeles: The Korea Times.

Yu, Eui-Young, Earl Phillips and Eun Sik Yang (eds.)
  1982   *Koreans in Los Angeles: Prospects and Promises.* Los Angeles: Center for Korean American and Korean Studies, California State University at Los Angeles.

Zenner, Walter
  1991   *Minorities in the Middle: A Cross-Cultural Analysis.* Albany, NY: State University of New York Press.